EASY RIDERS, ROLLING STONES

The Reverb series looks at the connections between music, artists and performers, musical cultures and places. It explores how our cultural and historical understanding of times and places may help us to appreciate a wide variety of music, and vice versa.

reverb-series.co.uk
Series editor: John Scanlan

Already published

The Beatles in Hamburg
Ian Inglis

Brazilian Jive: From Samba to Bossa and Rap
David Treece

Easy Riders, Rolling Stones: On the Road in America, from Delta Blues to '70s Rock
John Scanlan

Heroes: David Bowie and Berlin
Tobias Rüther

Jimi Hendrix: Soundscapes
Marie-Paule Macdonald

Neil Young: American Traveller
Martin Halliwell

Nick Drake: Dreaming England
Nathan Wiseman-Trowse

Remixology: Tracing the Dub Diaspora
Paul Sullivan

Tango: Sex and Rhythm of the City
Mike Gonzalez and Marianella Yanes

Van Halen: Exuberant California, Zen Rock'n'roll
John Scanlan

EASY RIDERS, ROLLING STONES

ON THE ROAD IN AMERICA, FROM DELTA BLUES TO '70S ROCK

JOHN SCANLAN

REAKTION BOOKS

Published by Reaktion Books Ltd
Unit 32, Waterside
44–48 Wharf Road
London N1 7UX, UK
www.reaktionbooks.co.uk

First published 2015

Copyright © John Scanlan 2015

Printed and bound in Great Britain by Bell & Bain, Glasgow

A catalogue record for this book is available from the British Library

ISBN 9 781 78023 529 5

CONTENTS

INTRODUCTION

Movement, travel and the reality of being 'on the road' have been central to the history of twentieth-century American music. As subject, metaphor and as the principal means of its spread and development, 'the road' has reflected important points of transition in blues, R&B and rock music – the subjects of this book – that in important ways have kept the music, as well as its performers, on the move towards new encounters and frontiers unknown.

But what is this thing that I will refer to as 'road music'? There are countless road *songs*, of course, and there are songs about 'roads' taken and routes in and out of despair and unhappiness. Some of the most well-known songs in the blues, rock 'n' roll and folk traditions could be cited as examples of 'road music', but these are not merely songs about driving, taking a trip or reaching a destination – rather, they are often primarily concerned with inward journeys that take some idea of the road, and mobility, as symbolic of broader sentiments and experiences. Even a partial list would extend to an unmanageable length, so accumulating the titles of songs pell-mell will not really get us any further into an understanding of what – at the end of the day – this 'road music' is all about.

But for anyone who has ever wondered what it is that has compelled this enduring fascination with 'the road', if not the very idea of movement, perhaps one example could serve, for the time being, to illustrate that the connection between a certain kind of American music and movement goes to the core of the relationship between experience, space and place. Mississippi Fred McDowell's recording of '61 Highway Blues' from 1959 captures the performance of a relatively old man – then in his fifties and, like so many of the Mississippi blues singers, then recently rediscovered – singing a song that he might have performed with more urgency and intent twenty or 30 years previously. This is not just a song that directly addresses the appeal of the openness of this particular highway – u.s. Highway 61 is the so-called 'blues highway' that runs the length of the country, cutting through its musical heartlands – as a unique kind of space with the power to fire the imagination. The song, in essence, sees in movement something beyond mere travel; something almost spiritual in the image of this fabled highway as the final destination for the restless, wandering musician of blues lore.

The song is also remarkable for the way that the rhythm of the music itself suggests that to be on the move is to enter another experiential dimension with its own temporality; its own 'music'. Mississippi Fred McDowell seems to knock a percussive and hypnotic sound out of his acoustic guitar that manages to achieve the *sensation* of something like wheels turning. The suggestion that presents itself to the listener – as he pines for that highway – is that his mind, if not his body, is set on forward motion. To the attentive listener, it is a sound compelling enough to temporarily disengage the mind and body from any other concerns, and to pull one into the 'space' it creates. This is, in many ways, 'ecstatic' music: it takes the performer and, at best, the listener, outside of themselves and into an unbounded space. And this, I want to suggest, is what is characteristic of road music: it is not merely concerned with music *of* the road, or with a kind of song whose subject is – variously – travel, escape, the possibility of movement or the urge towards self-transcendence, and so on. It is a kind of music that always seems to be seeking a way of escaping its confines, and eluding attempts to restrain the inherent freedom – whether personal or creative – that music, as a kind of pure and unfettered form of communication, seems to promise.

Travel and movement – and especially journeys towards unknown or surprising destinations – have, of course, been associated with romantic sentiments; with ideas about personal freedom, and with deep-rooted beliefs about the importance of the senses – of sense-experience and sensation – in artistic and creative acts of self-making. It is a fact that hints at the deeper roots of even the simplest desire to be on the road. And it perhaps might account for why certain kinds of music that are associated with movement, and with a kind of wandering impulse – in particular, the blues of the Mississippi Delta – represent a kind of art of *experience* that gives itself over to the moment.

At this point it is worth pausing to reflect on what I mean when I say that 'experience' is what this 'road music' seems to be about. To get philosophical about it, the notion of experience that has come to be understood as fundamental for grasping ideas of the 'self' in Western thinking is itself seen in terms of journeying. These might be journeys that are psychological in nature, or spiritual, or that elapse over time and distances actually travelled. But this 'temporally elongated' idea of experience points to ideas of self that arise from the 'integration of discrete moments of experience into a narrative whole or adventure'.[1] You are who you are, in other words, not only because of the 'distance' you have travelled in your life, but because you have understood yourself to have undertaken the journey of a life. That is to say, at the level of *experience* we are all – to a greater or lesser extent – 'on the road'.

In this sense, the mere idea of movement, which ends up being reflected in music in numerous ways, is often the consequence of slipping free from feelings of being controlled, confined or of being too tied to place and tradition. To be on the road was to perhaps find, in Jack Kerouac's words, a novel kind of freedom in which 'there was nowhere to go but everywhere'.[2] And it is within such a space of experience that road music materializes – in America.

Throughout history, humans have been 'on the road' in more than just the sense of spiritual journeying, and have been variously wayfarers, pilgrims, traders and tourists. They have been bought and sold as slaves and sent on journeys that landed them thousands of miles from their ancestral homes, and placed them into a seemingly permanent exile. They have been spiritual and mystical seekers of truth who saw that 'enlightenment' demanded that the hold of the physical world be transcended. In traditions ranging from those of ancient Greece (and the archetype of the hero's journey) to medieval Europe (and the idea of pilgrimage) and early modern Japan (the journey as a route to self-understanding), wandering has symbolized the human condition, and life itself is seen as a journey during which we may – at various points – take the form of exiles, spiritual or mystical seekers of greater truths, or drifters of indeterminate purpose.

The transformation of North America following waves of colonization and migration – and particularly the enforced migration of Africans – produced, over time, a cultural and musical distinctiveness. The American music that became blues, rock 'n' roll and other related forms is, in important ways, the result of geographical movement. Perhaps it is the result of movement above all else – particularly movement across the boundaries that separate people from their native forms of expression, and that consequently gives way to a new imaginative territory where the mixing of traditions and experiences become, in their own way, singularly American. But in the end, there is no music of, or on, the road without listeners. So what could it be that makes the idea of the road such a persistent theme in this music?

As listeners, we may actually be more likely to have very different experiences to those portrayed in road music. We live in places, in societies, that have been defined by their boundaries, that have made itinerancy an aberration, and in which we all seek the comfort of some kind of home. In other words, we do not – for the most part – desire to be on the road. Yet it is those of us who live settled lives who become the 'consumers' of the dreams of those who opt for, and create a culture from, a life of movement. We became the audience for generations of travelling musicians who remained in many ways detached from our kind of fixed and relatively stable lives. Perhaps it is because migration and movement is nonetheless a sedimented historical experience, an inheritance that marks most of us – even if only through our predecessors – that this 'road music' holds such appeal for us and seems in some ways to deserve to be called 'true', 'real' and 'authentic'.

Easy Riders, Rolling Stones does not present an inventory of songs about cars, trains, planes or – indeed – highways. To do that would be to end up detailing a somewhat dreary discography. Rather, it tells the more elusive story of the role that *the road* has played in the cultural imagination of America, and the music it produced and inspired in the twentieth century. It is a tale characterized by paradox and mystery. If the figures of itinerant wanderers we encounter here become almost stand-ins for ways of life that represent a kind of freedom that is now almost entirely foreign to those of us who look on in admiration or wonder, they are nonetheless – in terms of their cultural durability and influence – venerated as models of authenticity and originality; and often as avatars of a kind of truth-telling that goes to the core of what, although we might not be explicitly conscious of it, makes us human. And this is undoubtedly part of the appeal of road music, which both conveys a sense of movement and suggests that there is a vitality in being open to the possibilities presented by escaping the confines of normal experience. If the music discussed in these pages also, at times, suggests a kind of disorder and transgression that seems far from a contemporary listener's experience, the performers responsible for this nonetheless also inspire us – through their songs, performances and ways of living – to be true to our own selves, and to resist compromise. Why should this be the case? It is, arguably, because on the road the world is turned inside out: loss becomes discovery, the drifter becomes the artist, the stranger becomes familiar, the mundane becomes the source of ecstatic experience and law and society are supplanted by the kind of mores and habits appropriate, at other times, to frontier living.

This is a book about themes and about 'scenes' or moments. When I began thinking about this music of movement it became apparent that it existed as a particular phenomenon that had, due to structural changes in the music industry, peaked by the late 1970s or early 1980s, but which had roots in American music reaching back to the beginning of the twentieth century. By the mid-1970s, for instance, the record industry, as far as rock music was concerned, had settled into an economic model that seemed to push performers into a kind of semi-permanent exile. It wasn't unusual that the majority of a year would be spent on tour in support of an album, leaving only a few months left to write and record new music for a new album before the cycle began once again. To the artists and performers of this era who found themselves caught up in all of this – and more often than not, willingly so – such a life was, to all intents and purposes, an itinerant one. And given the way that the musician's experience was defined by movement and the experience of being rootless – however long it lasted – it is perhaps not surprising that life on the road gave rise to innumerable celebrations in song, as well as a wealth of literary and visual documents that came to represent its value as a form of cultural expression. Again, it is because life is a journey and the experience of the journey is what defines us, that these themes are so resonant.

But while the kind of celebration of life on the move that characterized rock music in the 1970s was not essentially new, it did take on new forms particular to its own time and place. Beyond the music and the musicians, the road had also become a way of life for a host of others – the record producers and promoters, the writers, photographers and documentary film-makers, the roadies, groupies and bootleggers – whose lives were not merely shaped by the music they were caught up in, but who in their own way contributed to how the entire culture of an era was viewed, both in its own time and later. They too, as we will see, submitted to the road and became central to the phenomenon as it reached its peak and then when it began to run out of momentum.

1 EARLY DELTA BLUES

> Country blues are fixed in time and space, language and
> custom; they are tied down to – and unerringly reflect –
> the geographical area, the local manners, and the exact
> vernacular of a specific place and person.
>
> Marshall W. Stearns, *Negro Blues and Field Hollers* (1962),
> LP liner notes

DOWNHOME

For a listener today, it is easy to imagine that perhaps the singer
was looking out towards some endless Delta flatland, reflecting on
the wide horizon that met the sky in the distance, and sometimes
never seemed to get closer no matter how far he walked, as he
sang: 'I'm going away to a world unknown / I'm worried now,
but I won't be worried long.'

But whatever relationship we might be tempted to draw
between the song of a wandering blues singer and the place in
which he plied his trade – a relationship that from a distance
seems to be laden with a certain emotional baggage – Charley
Patton's song 'Down the Dirt Road Blues' (1929) was presented
by Paramount, his record company, as something a little more
domestic and local than that scene of the small man in the vast
and foreboding landscape. For in its time it was a new tune by
a familiar character, perhaps encountered on previous records,
rather than something truly existential that – we might now say –
reflected a more profound sense of dissatisfaction with the world.
'He's had a lot of trouble at home and he's decided to hit the dirty,
dusty trail for parts unknown', the text of an advert for the record
published at that time read: 'He wants to forget everything and
go somewhere else, so he sings this novel Blues on his lazy mule
jogging him along the old dirt road.'[1]

This theme of escape, of being cast out or being compelled to hit the road, has its echo in countless blues songs – by Patton and others – and in the literature of black Americans in the South, where even the seemingly benign and open landscape that offers itself up to the traveller is a beguiling chimera. In J. J. Phillips's blues novel *Mojo Hand* (1966), the protagonist Eunice – a young woman besotted with the blues – dreams of leaving home for another life, of 'singing her leaving blues to a rising sun', but once set in motion, her illusions of freedom start to fall away.[2] 'The placating autumn rain had jested with the country and the people', she observes, looking from the window of a train:

> one would believe the life was as gentle as the deceivingly soft countryside . . . But it was as much a lie as the faces of the people, looking as if they were only capable of experiencing bland emotions when in reality violence was vulgarly raked from every scrap of life and exploded as suddenly and as effectively as the thunderstorms redundantly assailing the countryside.[3]

If the singer of the blues that emerged from this world was 'going away to a world unknown', we as listeners today, separated from their world by time and influenced in our perceptions by history and historical representations, are no less confronted by a music that seems to exist under an 'aura of mystery and misinformation'.[4] But, more than that, it captures a kind of experience that is, essentially, incommunicable to the outsider.

Having said that, what one can see and hear is that the universality of this kind of sentiment – 'to forget everything and go somewhere else' – runs through the country blues that came out of the Mississippi Delta in the early part of the twentieth century. The relationship of this music to space and travel casts some light on the lives of what blues historian Francis Davis

termed 'loners', who sang of their experience of life and of a
desire to remain free.[5] But such a desire did not merely express
the importance attached to personal freedom; it was, rather,
motivated by the need to cut loose from the constraints of a
society ruled by caste, and by the new 'Jim Crow' segregationist
laws, validated by the u.s. Supreme Court in 1896 and enacted
in the southern states, which rolled back the equalities that had
seemed to be guaranteed to African Americans after the 1875 Civil
Rights Act. The laws enforced extreme restrictions on the freedoms
of black Americans in the South, and barred them from 'any form
of economic competition with whites'. Their freedom, it seems,
was found only in ideas of movement, travel and transcendence:
on the road.[6]

Charley Patton, born in the 1880s, at a time when there still
existed the hope of some kind of equality, lived through these
changes. He was a pioneer of a particular kind of blues music
that originated in, and came to be associated with, the Mississippi
Delta, the lowland area between the Mississippi and Yazoo rivers.
The music was what some described as 'downhome . . . back to
the root . . . it came from the country, the fields and the shacks
and the towns that weren't but wide spaces in the highway'.[7]
And it can sound as desolate and open as that suggests, calling
up mental images of a scarred land of wooden and corrugated
metal shacks, and trees that seem to have been stripped to the
bark by punishing winds.

This kind of blues was rough and uncompromising, distinct
from the blues of New Orleans, which contained jazz and ragtime
elements. Nor was it musically like the blues associated with the
popular female singers of the day, such as Bessie Smith – singers
who essentially fronted jazz bands and performed 'blues' vocals.
What the various kinds of blues had in common was the lyrical
and verse elements, organized around the repetition of 'identical
or near-identical lines followed by a line that offers a comment or

response'.[8] This was influenced by the call-and-response structure of spirituals and field hollers, which tended to consist of dialogues between two individuals or groups, but which in blues became an 'internalized, contemplative mode of self-questioning and confession'.[9]

Musically, Delta blues was often relentless and percussive – with, some say, antecedents in the storytelling of West African *griot*, whose songs were accompanied by drumming, hand-clapping, steel-string instruments and call-and-response singing – and with the steel-strung guitar as usually the single source of rhythm and harmonic accompaniment to the voice.[10] Sometimes the singer would dig in to those strings hard, bang the body of the guitar with his fist, or slap the strings on the neck to create a rhythm. And the voices, above all, were idiosyncratic, seemingly in touch with the truth, channelling pain and a yearning for freedom; a 'deep, heavy, serious metaphysical baggage' not heard in other blues.[11]

These blues were the burden and the object of contemplation that sent numerous rootless men out onto the road in an attempt to escape their woes. And when Robert Johnson – in the 1930s – sang of the need to keep moving, of blues *falling down like hail*, he may have been expressing a general sense of oppression felt by blacks in the South; a sense that was perhaps intensified for travelling singers who may have been viewed as strangers or outsiders anyway, just by virtue of the way they blew in and out of town. Always mindful of 'the ever-pressurizing white gaze', and the 'periodic eruptions of ritualized mob violence', Adam Gussow suggests these blues are also 'a way of expressing the *feeling*' that the 'soul-deadening network of oppressions produces'.[12]

It was music that had perhaps been around since the turn of the century, but which was preserved in recordings that were made in the 1920s and '30s, sometimes field recordings and other times commercial recordings, aimed at a black audience by record companies who released on 78 rpm discs they labelled 'race records' – music by black performers for the African American consumer, a booming market in the new phonographic age. It was a music, however, that almost became extinct until it was rediscovered in the late 1950s and more widely brought to public awareness by the 1960s rock musicians who took elements of this blues and amplified it, and tried to live according to its visions of freedom and movement. For all their differences in presentation – the lone voice with the acoustic guitar versus the amplified rock band – they both relied, as Stephen Calt noted, 'on the same principle of rhythmic tension, created by establishing an underlying rhythmic pulse and then embroidering it with syncopation'.[13]

The 'aura of novelty' in this music to those 1960s musicians who fell under its sway was partly due to the fact that it was not the popular music of its day – many sides released by now-legendary Delta blues artists had been 'commercial duds' when marketed at the target black audience. When the British rock trio Cream (Eric Clapton, Jack Bruce and Ginger Baker) performed their version of 'Spoonful' – based on a record by Howlin' Wolf that was partially based on Charley Patton's 'A Spoonful Blues' of 1929 – the aggressive, unrelenting and ominous quality that a Delta singer would bring to a song was remade into something unique to its own time and place. A pummelling guitar and bass riff here establishes a syncopated rhythm that exists merely as the point of departure for a rhythmic punctuation that drives *downwards*, with a force that takes the often ominous sounding combination of the blues voice and rhythmic accompaniment and turns it into some kind of a sonic cataclysm.

The influence of the Delta singers on later generations was also, in part, a result of the 'potent mystique' that envelops the ostensible subject of the Delta blues song. They sang songs that alluded to the numerous torments that assailed a bluesman on the road, lending their music an undeniable existential potency

that could be communicated across time and distance. Many of
the singers seemed to be in permanent exile from the norms and
values of a society that, in the 1920s and '30s, was as much of a trap
as antebellum slavery. The life of many of these blues singers at that
time was an itinerant one; days, months and years spent travelling
between towns and settlements, cotton plantations and work
camps all over the South to perform and to make a living. They
were representative of a time and place that seemed, to some, to
be strangely out of kilter with the modern world. The songs of
Charley Patton – the pivotal figure in the history of the Delta blues
– might be taken to reflect this kind of fugitive existence, always on
the move from something or other. He did, after all, leave behind
seven ex-wives (he died when he was still married to wife number
eight, fellow blues singer Bertha Lee). As John Fahey notes, the
impression one has from listening to the lyrics of Patton's songs,
with their 'strange, weird, even ghastly emotional states', is of
someone who is subject to forces beyond his control:

> women, trains, the fates, prison, the Law, even those strange,
> ambivalent feelings which seek to control him when he thinks
> about his mother. And travel. He is always singing about
> escape routes.[14]

It was in 1903 that W. C. Handy – a black orchestra leader
based in Clarksdale, Mississippi – encountered Delta blues for the
first time, when he was awoken by a strange-sounding music as he
waited for a long-overdue train in Tutwiler, Mississippi. It was the
sound of a pocketknife being slid over the steel strings of a guitar
by 'a black man in ragged clothes' – creating the keening, often
haunted sound we now know as 'slide guitar' – that captivated
him, he later recalled.[15] Handy represented a different musical
world entirely; one where the kind of 'simple repetition' found in
Delta blues 'could not be adequate' and where any music that was

'not written down' was inferior.[16] Robert Palmer speculated in
Deep Blues that the circumstances of this meeting may have left
Handy in the kind of woozy delirium that made it sound like the
weirdest sound he had ever heard:

> Tutwiler, which is fifteen minutes southeast of Clarksdale on
> Highway 49, had only a few hundred citizens in the early 1900s,
> and in the middle of the night the train depot, with closed-up
> stores in forbidding lines on either side of it, must have been a
> lonely place. Handy could probably hear the ghostly rustle of
> cypress and willow trees that were watered by nearby Hobson
> Bayou. The darkened stores, the trees bending and swaying
> over the track, a stray dog or two – it wasn't much to see, and
> Handy had seen it all innumerable times.[17]

And then the surprise of the weird music heard for the first
time. Sometimes it echoed the singer's voice, adding emphasis to
a particular word or lyrical image, and at other times responded to
it, as if the singer was in dialogue with the voice of the instrument.
It is the sound we can still hear today on Charley Patton's recording
of 'A Spoonful Blues', where he not only uses the slide on the strings
to voice the word 'spoonful' but develops a multiple-voicing
effect, comprised of his 'customary singing voice, a womanish
falsetto, a lower speaking voice, and the voice of the slider'.[18]

This kind of improvisation with only the most rudimentary
of instrumentation was, to a sophisticated musician like Handy,
something that seemed totally alien, something that opened a
crack in the surface of reality, exposing a past, and a world, that
was still alive in a time of machines and railroads, which had
shrunk the whole country but had not tamed the tensions that
existed deep within the South; a place that became strange all
over again. Handy, with his musician's ears, saw the novelty
of this blues form, stripped bare to the essentials of voice and

steel-string guitar. At the beginning of the 1960s, a period in which this music was revived, one expert remarked that the music was 'archaic', but in an entirely positive sense. These were songs 'sung by men usually to the accompaniment of a stringed instrument (guitar preferred); and they are gnarled, rough-hewn, and eminently uncommercial'.[19] But others, on first encountering the blues, may have had an experience more like that of John Grimes, the hero of James Baldwin's *Go Tell It on the Mountain*, who recognized for the first time not the apparent newness of this sound, but a different kind of truth to the reality he had been living with:

> He had heard it all his life, but it was only now that his ears were opened to this sound that came from the darkness, that could only come from darkness . . . it was the sound of rage and weeping which filled the grave, rage and weeping from time set free, but bound now in eternity.[20]

It would not be untrue to say that the South would come to represent the persistent memory of wrongs that could not be adequately corrected, and the land where the blues was born seemed more extreme than anywhere else. The Delta, in particular, was, James Cobb wrote, 'the most Southern place on earth . . . an isolated, time-warped enclave whose startling juxtapositions of white affluence and black poverty' seemed to present 'the Old South legacy preserved in microcosm'.[21]

INTO THE DELTA

What was this place, this environment that spawned blues singers like Charley Patton, Son House and Tommy Johnson? The Mississippi Delta has often been described as a 'primordial' landscape, a place that seems to exist outside of time – 'the world

Abandoned cabins on a plantation in the Mississippi Delta, 1937.

Noah might have glimpsed after the flood'.[22] The first settlers
to attempt to make a home in the area that would come to be
known as the Delta arrived by steamboat. Through the thick
swamplands, they found an area that might be suitable for
settlement. But it had to be tamed and brought under control,
and the forests that seemed to crowd visibility had to be felled.

Occupying an area between Memphis, Tennessee, to the
north and Vicksburg, Mississippi, to the south, and bounded
by the Mississippi River to the west and Highway 51 as it runs
south from Memphis to Jackson, Mississippi, to the east, the
Delta was, until the time of the U.S. Civil War, a swampland that
would eventually be drained for – primarily – cotton farming, and
opened up by the incursion of railroads. It was a rich alluvial
plain, apparently flat as far as the eye could see, and with a
'jungle-like vegetation and climactic unpredictability' that stalled

its eventual settlement.[23] But its susceptibility to flooding ensured that it remained a prospect for the adventurous planter, as 'flood after flood spread blankets of rich alluvium over accumulating layers of decomposing vegetation', meaning that – from human interference or not – 'the Delta's soil only grew richer'.[24]

The Delta, for many, also seems to be a land beyond time, for very human and historical reasons: the sense that the South that is associated with the Delta represents a bygone world of an America that was supposed to have been left behind by progress. It is where old ways, outmoded ideas and a deep-seated conservatism could still be found. As is so often the case with unspoken or unconscious habits and customs that are peculiar to particular times and places, it takes an outsider – an emigrant, even – to see the old ways as new and baffling, and to pick up on the nuances in the culture that reveal some kind of deeper truth. As a young professor moving south to the University of Mississippi in Oxford in the 1980s, James Cobb was struck by the way people related to this place:

> I soon noticed that in Mississippi one spoke not of going to Clarksdale, Greenville, or Greenwood, but of traveling 'into the Delta,' the implication being that of passage back in time, to a setting that – if such a thing were possible – seemed even more southern than the rest of the state.[25]

But back in time, going back to the period in which the first planters arrived, the Deep South of such perceptions was a difficult place to settle, seemingly inhospitable to human endeavours; a 'land heavily forested and studded with cypress swamps and dense canebrakes', and where 'alligators slithered through the murky bottoms and panthers stalked deer among the cane'.[26] It was a frontier land, and – for so many – the land that could never really be home. Yet within the American experience, which is one of emigration, what the Deep South illustrates is that the state of mind of being in a new place, or some inhospitable world far from home, is relative to place, not only in a simplistic or lateral way (being far flung from one's birthplace, for instance), but in what it means socially and economically to actually belong, or be at one, with place. Those who were the descendants of slaves in a world still ruled by the same people it always had been ruled by, even after emancipation, were no less homeless than they had always been. During the depression of the 1930s, for instance, when the hobo life was rife among many who were down on their luck, 'many young Blacks preferred to join the growing army of homeless drifters' rather than the work camps that had been set up as part of government initiatives like the Civilian Conservation Corps.[27]

And so, depending on the upheavals and travails of living on the cusp of modernity, which the South was – this was a world, after all, that underwent huge changes in the century following the end of the Civil War in 1865 – the sense of who belonged and who was outcast would change. That well-known air of Southern sentimentality, known as '(I Wish I Was in) Dixie', for instance, was recast during the Civil War as 'The Song of the Exile', a comfort for the dislodged confederates pining for the *certainties* of an Old South that they hoped might survive unchanged in the face of the modern wreckers of tradition who had proclaimed their world obsolete. The song would subsequently appear as a reminder to the subjugated descendants of the slaves that the ideology of the South had deep and sentimental roots that could not be easily severed. It was a place that continued to lend itself to partisan commitments and partial perspectives, even when they seemed to fly in the face of the facts. 'The architects of the New South', the post-Reconstruction South that would eventually give rise to the blues of the Delta and beyond, 'had embellished not just the past but the present as well' and professed the triumph of social progress and the riches of economic prosperity that were based on a booming cotton trade.[28] The South, indeed, seems to lend itself to the creation of prodigious myths of origin and history. Against this background in the Delta – in the 1920s, '30s and '40s – many of the most durable figures in the history of American music would be found.

The life of Charley Patton, the first influential figure in the spread of the blues within the Delta according to most accounts, was fairly typical of the kind of wandering existence that playing the blues made possible. It was to the Delta that Charley Patton's family migrated when he was in his teens, moving from southern Mississippi to take advantage of the much-trumpeted opportunities in the north. And it was on the Dockery Plantation, an 'immense, forty-square-mile' area off Highway 61 and close to Clarksdale, where he grew up within a population of 'over 500 black laborers [who] cleared new land for cotton'.[29] It was there that Patton would become an accomplished performer, influenced initially by some older musicians who lived at Dockery's.[30] It was there, or around there, that the blues seems to have originated, with a number of younger musicians, such as Tommy Johnson and Son House, coming through and taking a cue from Patton and his sometime partner Willie Brown.[31] Tommy Johnson's own 'Big Road Blues' of 1928 was a song not only about being pushed out onto the road, but one that developed through his travels and performances to take on new elements that deviated from the recorded version.[32] In its general sentiment of escaping a troubled life, however temporarily, it arguably shared much in common with Patton's 'Down the Dirt Road Blues'.

What, then, was one to make of the sound of this music, rising up from some unknown depths; those voices that 'sounded peculiar and striking, muffled and contorted' by the medium that, in its scratched or worn state, allowed them to rise again?[33] As Francis Davis suggests, listening on record when separated by the distance of time and space could, on its own, lead the listener into a highly charged imaginative space; one – for instance – where 'the rhythmic weave of Patton's voice and guitar' became 'so compelling, so primeval, that even the most level-headed blues scholars' felt tempted 'to conjecture a mythic past for him'.[34]

While Patton has been the object of 'considerable fascination and considerable myth-making', there are certain details about his life that have only recently 'begun to come into focus'.[35] He spent his earliest years moving between the towns of Bolton and Edwards, before arriving at the Dockery Plantation in the northern Delta. Between these places and Vicksburg in the southern Delta, as David Evans has written, Patton established a network of locations connected to his extended family that remained fairly constant on his itinerary throughout his life:

> His sister lived on Dockery's, as did his father and mother and another sister and brother for many years. At other times they lived nearby in places like Mound Bayou, Renova and Blaine. Charley himself is frequently described as living in Mound Bayou and nearby Merigold as well as at Dockery's. Between Bolton and Edwards and at Vicksburg he had aunts and uncles and cousins as well as his grandmother in Vicksburg.[36]

And from the Mississippi hill country bordering the Delta in the East, which in the words of American writer Rick Bass 'attaches itself like a long muscle to either side of Highway 51', further, and lighter or less 'existential', variants of what outsiders would think of as a kind of American 'folk' music peculiar to this part of the South would be found embodied in the songs of 'Mississippi' John Hurt, who recorded in the late 1920s but remained undiscovered until the late 1950s when some blues connoisseurs 'discovered' him – living in the same place he had always lived. Blues was, of course, found elsewhere in the southern United States at the time, especially in Texas and

Louisiana, but the wellspring of the 'road music' that undergoes a transformation once it escapes the Delta – through the 1950s to the 1970s – is the music that came from this time and place, and was communicated to the outside world through the routes and channels that formed the ways in and out of its past.

RAMBLIN' MEN

What was communicated to the outside world was more than just the music. The stories that were told of figures such as Charley Patton only seemed to multiply the mysteries of the blues, a state of affairs that in itself would be the source of an ever-greater attraction. It was said that due to his unusual looks he might have had Mexican or perhaps Native American origins. 'Patton', Francis Davis suggests, 'must have looked "light" to blacks, and "dark" to whites.'[37] He released records under a pseudonym, 'The Masked Marvel', further adding to the confusion. One rumour that had evidently taken shape in the years following his death in 1934 was that Patton had been murdered – some said that he had his throat cut by a jealous husband, others that he met a fate more fitting of a blues singer who tarried with the dark side: Gayle Dean Wardlow, one of the most indefatigable early blues researchers, was told that Patton 'was struck and instantly killed by a lightning bolt'. Without any kind of evidence to verify the actual cause of death, it was the kind of story that would attach itself to 'those who followed the Devil in singing "his" blues'.[38]

Patton, who would become known as the 'King of the Delta Blues Singers', was a figure so elusive to his own kin, so much on the margins of the expectations of conventional society, that he was apparently referred to as 'X' by his stepfather. He was an 'enigma', John Fahey wrote, 'who wore a mask, used pseudonyms, had many voices, many styles and, yes, many wives . . . this actor, hypnotist, clown, preacher, wealthy magician'.[39] Those seeking to

uncover his identity would return again and again to the only
known photograph of the bluesman – a portrait taken to promote
one of his records. And through the mists of time and myth, this
image seemed all the more remarkable for the fact that Patton
had 'sat long enough in one spot to be photographed at all'.[40] For
a long time all that could be seen of Patton was his head, which
seemed to confirm the stories of contemporaries that he was of
mixed race, and perhaps more parts Native American than
anything else. But such evidence provided a possible route back
into that time:

> Some people who look at this photo think they see madness
> or fear or a bad hangover in Patton's dazed stare and slightly
> parted lips. But this is probably discomfort at being
> photographed – nothing more. Other people read cool
> menace into Patton's expressionless mug, but this is a
> deduction based on the gravel of his recorded voice and
> on his reputation as a woman-beater and braggart.[41]

In time, though, the full portrait surfaced, showing the singer
seated in a photographer's studio, well dressed with bow tie and
spats, and cradling his guitar in his lap as he held an upside-down
chord shape on the neck.

The identification of the blues with the dark side – and of the
blues as 'the Devil's music' – has long been a source of fascination
for enthusiasts and scholars alike. This association also reflected,
more generally, aspects of the culture of the South, particularly
among 'black Baptists and Pentecostals', who referred to the blues
(and to jazz) in those terms.[42] Patton, and some of his Mississippi
blues associates and contemporaries, purveyors of this 'Devil's
music', would swing over to the 'other side', either preaching or
performing church songs, or both, in the case of Son House and
Skip James.[43] Robert Wilkins, who played around the Delta with

Charley Patton,
c. 1929.

Patton and House in the 1920s and early 1930s, and was later
brought to wider public attention when The Rolling Stones
covered his song 'Prodigal Son' on their 1968 album *Beggars
Banquet*, was another – although a different character to Patton,
mild-mannered and tee-total – who went further and gave up the
blues for the church, becoming an ordained minister in 1950.[44]
Wilkins, like so many of the blues singers of this time, had
actually recorded numerous songs whose key theme was
movement, with titles such as 'Rolling Stone' and 'Holy Ghost
Train', among others.

 While its subject is a straightforward rendering of the biblical
parable of rebellion, failure and remorseful return, 'Prodigal Son'

is a song that allows us to get closer to understanding what the meaning of this label, 'the Devil's music', reveals about the lives and beliefs of Delta blues musicians, and also about some of the more persistent myths of the blues. It is the tale of a young man tempted into what we might call evil ways; a thief who steals from his own father and trades family life for a life on the road, but ultimately returns home to seek forgiveness.

There is this sense, then, that to choose the life of the wandering blues singer is to take a deviant route, the path of 'evil' – that is not to say, as some debunkers who are keen on sweeping away the mythologies of the blues suggest, a literal pact with the Devil. To choose a life of uncertainty and, in all likelihood, danger, over the settled, hard-working life that was the Christian way, is to deviate from the path of goodness. The blues was also associated with all manner of fast living and ungodly pursuits – a veritable underworld of promiscuous sex, drinking, here-today-gone-tomorrow hell-raising, gambling and generally living the life of a drifter.

John Fahey, the musician-collector who claims to have been the first person to go looking for Charley Patton or anyone who knew him, back in 1958, was able to quickly find that the singer remained well known for his music, although the details of his life were sometimes hazy and already infused with an element of myth. People he spoke to about Patton

> remembered that he drank a lot and *lived a rough life* (i.e., he was not very religious) and that his last record was 'There Ain't No Grave Gonna Hold My Body Down', which he recorded just a few days before being stabbed to death or poisoned by a jealous woman.[45]

There was no such recording and, although a relatively young man in his early forties, Patton – it was later discovered – died of heart failure. But living the 'rough life' was common for many. Tommy Johnson, like so many others, travelled all over Mississippi, playing at parties, in barrelhouses or even on the street for loose change. He was an alcoholic who, in desperation, would drink the jellied fuel used for lighting a traveller's portable stove – a product called Sterno. This was the so-called 'canned heat' of his 'Canned Heat Blues'.

But the belief that blues singers were in league with the Devil, which was an aspect of the style of living that was commonly associated with the itinerant, rootless life of blues singers, was also underpinned by other aspects of the folklore of the South. The characterization of the blues as the 'the Devil's music' had much to do with the persistence and credibility of more general beliefs influenced by the fragmented 'system of magic and medicine formulated from an admixture of cultural beliefs' and known as 'hoodoo'.[46] Such beliefs ascribed magical transformative powers to places, objects and local cultural practices.[47]

One of the most persistent myths that swirls around the Delta blues has attached itself, in particular – although not alone – to Robert Johnson; the artist who hadn't made any recordings until after Charley Patton's death in 1934, but who would be dubbed 'King of the Delta Blues Singers' by canny record company men in the 1960s. The Robert Johnson myth concerns the road, or – to be more specific – a certain understanding of the dangers and opportunities found in the life of the travelling musician. It conveys widely held beliefs about what can happen to the traveller at the intersection of two diverging roads or paths – at a crossroads, in other words, which in African American folk beliefs symbolically represents the meeting of two worlds: the worlds of the living and the dead.

In *O Brother, Where Art Thou?* (2000), Joel and Ethan Coen's movie set in the Mississippi Delta during the 1930s, three escaped convicts trying to find their way home give a ride to a bluesman, Tommy Johnson, who had been waiting at a crossroads all night, he

'Willie Brown' waits at the crossroads in *Crossroads*, the 1986 Hollywood reworking of the Johnson myth.

said, 'to sell' his 'soul to the Devil'. The existence of the crossroads of blues legend has been the subject of much ridicule and speculation, not to mention an entertaining Hollywood film, *Crossroads* (1986), that follows an old bluesman on his journey back to the crossroads to have his pact with 'the Devil' torn up. Travellers keen to either confirm or dispel the myth have gone in search of these crossroads. The location of the crossroads used in the Hollywood movie, for instance, was Beulah, Mississippi, located on U.S. Highway 1. The choice of this location perhaps betrays the film's debt to British rock band Cream's recording of 'Crossroads' from 1968, which – in lyrical terms – was a combination of two Robert Johnson songs, 'Cross Road Blues' and 'Traveling Riverside Blues'. Cream's 'Crossroads' imported the geography of 'Traveling Riverside Blues' into the myth that sprung up around the story told in 'Cross Road Blues'. Beulah is close to the town of Rosedale, which features in 'Traveling Riverside Blues', but in the Cream version appears to be where the friend who might come to Robert Johnson's aid – Willie Brown – could be found.

Willie Brown returns with young guitar player Eugene, to call off his deal with Legba (the Devil), *Crossroads* (1986).

As a location for the mythical crossroads, whatever the truth was, Beulah seemed like the 'perfect place', according to a recent tourist guide to the Delta's 'holy' blues places:

> Not only do you have a real Mississippi Delta dirt-road crossroads, but you also get a cemetery, some burnt old trees, and the remains of a church at the spot. Dogs on surrounding farms tend to howl at night.[48]

But others, also with eyes set on the tourists of the present, say the location of the fabled crossroads was at the intersection of highways 49 and 61, the main arteries that run the length of the Mississippi Delta – just around Clarksdale, in fact – where the Delta blues was said to originate, and where Charley Patton, Tommy Johnson and countless others probably found themselves on many occasions. It is an area that is now part of the Mississippi blues tourist industry, complete with its own Blues Museum and other attractions.[49]

2 JOURNEYS INTO THE PAST: DELTA MYTHS AND REALITIES

BOUND FOR HOME

In *O Brother, Where Art Thou?*, Joel and Ethan Coen's film set in the Deep South of Depression-era America, with a story that could have been an extended take on Charley Patton's 'High Water Everywhere', Ulysses Everett McGill (played by George Clooney) is, like his ancient and mythical counterpart in Homer's *Odyssey*, a man of cunning – 'driven to wander far and wide . . . in his struggles to preserve his life and bring his comrades home'.[1] It is a movie that has been as equally remarked upon for its jumbled and sanitized presentation of Old South clichés (lynch mobs, chain gangs, KKK rallies, grubby racial politics) as for its stunning visual quality and loopy comedy. Yet it could also be seen as a story of the hero's descent into a veritable underworld of life-threatening encounters and unwelcome challenges that must be overcome – a version, in other words, of the mythical journey. In many such hero myths, David Adams Leeming notes, 'the hero, like the dying god, descends into death and in returning brings great boons to his or her culture. Often the gift is a new crop – corn or wheat – or some new spiritual knowledge.'[2] But what McGill and his cronies bring back, so to speak, is music – music that the Coens represent as a means of overcoming racial conflict in one of the final scenes, when the runaway convicts find themselves performing before an election rally to an audience that resists the entreaties of the local KKK leader to lynch the musicians for miscegenation.

Scenes from *O Brother, Where Art Thou?* (2000): A chain gang
of prisoners from Parchman Farm (top); the leader of the escaped
convicts, Ulysses Everett McGill (middle); on the run from the law, the
escapees pick up bluesman Tommy Johnson at a crossroads (bottom).

If some elements of the film are fanciful distortions of a reality that make the past it casts light on easily digestible, the music nonetheless squarely roots it in the Mississippi Delta; it is a road movie that has music as its central theme. Delta blues, mountain music, prison songs and field hollers – viewed from the present perspective it portrays an essential truth: the power of music is that it is a phenomenon that can overcome differences, surmount obstacles and, not insignificantly, act as a conduit for cultural memory, carrying the listener into the time-space of a bygone age. As a Library of Congress primer on 'Negro Blues and Field Hollers' from 1962 stated, the music of the Delta seemed 'fixed in time and space, language and custom'. The blues, in particular, 'are tied down to – and unerringly reflect – the geographical area, the local manners, and the exact vernacular of a specific place'.[3]

The Mississippi we see in *O Brother* is a place steeped in the kind of American music that was the result of decades and centuries of cross-fertilization of folk currents that had their origins in the songs and music of Africa and the British Isles. It is the music Harry Smith described as 'American Folk Music' in his landmark *Anthology* of records of the 1920s and '30s, first released in the early 1950s and successfully re-issued for the digital age almost 50 years later.[4] And it is music that brings McGill, the hero – playing out the mythic 'hero's journey', no less – back into the arms of his estranged wife and children.

In this loose transposition of elements of a well-worn myth to a time and place that might seem no less distant than the ancient world is to contemporary viewers, we see not a faithful rendering of the Homeric epic, but a version of that tale as an 'enduring myth, a story that is buried deep in our culture and emerges in all kinds of new forms'.[5] In a sense, what the film's depiction of the South reveals is that our understanding of place – especially when its history has become fused with a music and culture that has since (as we will see) been loosened from time and place – is always informed by a mixture of the real and the ideal, the factual and the fanciful. And in a strange way, like so many of the songs that constitute this body of American music, the film was not aiming for realism so much as for 'an imagined world where all those things intersect – real people and made up people'.[6] As one academic has remarked, *O Brother* could be seen as simply a 'purposeful mis-remembering', or an 'artistic pastiche' that evokes the period, or the way it has been represented in Hollywood films, but which has much in common with the strategies that seem to characterize other phenomena of contemporary cultural memory, such as historical re-enactments of past ways of life (the whole culture and heritage shebang).[7] Blues scholar-pedants, of course, abound, and today, perhaps having run out of new artists to discover, they seem to focus their attention on overturning every myth that had brought the blues to life for listeners far removed from it, in a search for 'facts'. It was precisely the fact that figures such as Charley Patton were so out of reach, and their lives were so devoid of the facts and evidence that normally construct a biography, that they became so imbued with a kind of weight and mystery that adds immeasurably to the perception of the music as the sound of a lost world.

As our hero and his two companions are chased and harried around Mississippi in what appears to be 1927, for they are caught up in the Great Flood of that year, they seem to be popping up all over the state. When we meet them, they have escaped from a chain gang on Parchman Farm (the State Penitentiary) in the north – in Delta country – the place they will be drawn back to repeatedly on this strange, circuitous journey home. Indeed, viewers looking for geographical accuracy in the film will soon be confused, as our heroes seem to crop up in a succession of unlikely locations, bouncing from the far south to the north and back again. The compression of time and space makes it clear that

A view of Mississippi, during the flood of May 1927.

the geography and historical events represented in *O Brother* are more incidental than actual – a mere backdrop for the story, a kind of 'fictional micro-climate'.[8]

Its relation to the actual, indeed, recalls Patton's song 'High Water Everywhere' about the flood of 1927, in which his 'tangled itinerary' took him

> all up and down the Delta during the winter and spring of 1927, when the region was buffeted by tornadoes, rocked by earthquakes, drenched with the heaviest rains anyone could remember, and finally all but washed away by the rampaging Mississippi, which overflowed its banks and inundated the lowlands.[9]

And like such songs, the film – in its use of music, language and scenery – mixes its various elements in order to try and evoke some kind of truth about time and place, creating a compelling visual tableau within which the real, the fictional and the mythic come to life as some kind of sepia-toned world that is straight out of an alluring picture book.

Historical figures from the period (in some cases, only approximately) flit in and out of the picture. A bluesman named Tommy Johnson – there was, of course, a real Tommy Johnson who lived and played in the Delta in the 1920s – is carried along with McGill and his two fellow escaped convicts, Pete and Delmar, for much of the film. At one point, as they are hunted down by a search party, Tommy, probably fearing a lynching, lights out on his own, soon after they rob a bank with George 'Babyface' Nelson. Towards the film's conclusion, the opportunistic politician who pardons them of their crimes, Pappy O'Daniel, is an echo of a real figure of that name, although he is displaced in the movie from Texas to Mississippi.

More remarkable than these collisions of real and invented characters is the way that the damp and humid climate of Mississippi is transformed into a parched landscape: the lush green of the waist-high crops and swampy forests the convicts escape through is transformed into a pale yellowish hue, heightening the sense of heat, perhaps in reference to the scorched landscapes of the dustbowl era during which the movie is set. While *O Brother* evokes the poverty of the Depression through its visual touches, it equally seems to suggest a place that is, in many ways, in keeping with the music that sprung from Mississippi – the blues, country and folk music that would find its way into mainstream rock 'n' roll during the second half of the century. This was the music of 'the old weird America' as Greil Marcus has described it, redolent of a history that seemed still – even by the twentieth century – to be peopled by 'slaves, indentured servants, convicts, hustlers, adventurers, the ambitious and the greedy, the fleeing and the hated', and so on.[10] This America – the sense of place as seen through a pervasive musical culture – constitutes a world that is at once strange and familiar; it is both of the modern world and yet seemingly endlessly produces, through the songs and recordings that remain always in our present, the spirit of a time and place that is as archaic as anything that ancient myth might throw up.

And while this character, Ulysses Everett McGill, becomes a cipher through which we glimpse this now strange world that exists somewhere between dream and reality, he and his fellow travellers also seem undeniably universal figures within the context of the history of the continent; they are a kind of embodiment of the American experience as it had been for so many in the 300 years that had gone before. All of which is to say that the American experience has been one of emigration, exile and displacement. It has encompassed mass migrations, both enforced and voluntary, exploration and colonization, and a restlessness and questing that takes some kind of ideal form in visions of a freedom that may only be found after landscapes have been conquered, personal limits tested and horizons expanded. 'The unforeseen openings of the American situation', according to Daniel Boorstin, enjoined a will to embrace mobility and the possibilities of transformation.[11] 'No prudent man dared to be too certain of exactly who he was or what he was about; everyone had to be prepared to become someone else.'[12] McGill, like his namesake Ulysses, is nothing if not adaptable to new situations.

LAND OF EXILE

But for one group of Americans, the African slaves transported to the southern states of the American Republic over a period of some two centuries, the experience of exile has been more scarring than among any other group. In terms of the black African American experience, the trauma and memory of slavery produces what Paul Gilroy terms a 'double consciousness'; one that impels the culture that is expressed in some of the most singular examples of the blues, and in particular the Mississippi Delta blues.[13] Through the blues – and later forms of music that were born, in one way or another, of the legacy of the 'Black Atlantic' – historical experience is turned around in songs that 'evoke and affirm a condition in which the negative meanings given to the enforced movement of blacks are somehow transposed', so that

> what was initially felt to be a curse – the curse of homelessness or the curse of enforced exile – gets repossessed. It becomes affirmed and is reconstructed as the basis of a privileged standpoint from which certain useful and critical perceptions about the modern world become more likely.[14]

In *O Brother*, we see Tommy Johnson as a kind of aimless drifter who ends up in cahoots with people on the run from the law; but it seems clear from his campfire rendition of Skip James's 'Hard Time Killing Floor Blues' that what is chasing him is something more haunting – it is history and memory and the elusive prospect of freedom – which the song captures in an image of unremitting suffering. It is a life projected outwards in order to reveal how consigned blacks were to one crushing blow after another on the 'killing floor' of Southern society (it was a well-used term for slaughterhouse). In performance, the song was cut through with the haunted sighs of mournful hummed passages that evoked a sense of fatalism whose only reprieve seemed to be in the comfort offered by the repetition of the song's lilting melody.[15]

While Tommy Johnson never actually recorded this song, it is entirely likely that he knew and even performed it. Skip James, the

writer of the song, was one of the earliest of the Delta blues
singers, and like more well-known contemporaries and near-
contemporaries, his songs would be resurrected in the 1960s, as
white rock 'n' roll musicians (primarily from England initially)
mined the extant recordings of the 1920s and '30s for inspiration
and in search of songs that could be recast by highly amplified
rock bands. Unlike his contemporaries though, Skip James lived
to see the revival of his songs, which perhaps explains why he
never attained the mythic, otherworldly aura of Charley Patton
and Robert Johnson – both often referred to as 'King of the
Delta Blues', as previously mentioned'.[16] But like those two,
and so many others, James conformed to the idea of the restless,
itinerant blues singer of the early decades of the century, perhaps
even acquiring the name Skip – according to his biographer
Stephen Calt – from his 'footloose existence' or propensity
to skip town for one reason or another. Beyond that, his life
was simply a reflection of the fact that most blues singers
of the time were 'itinerants' or 'rolling stones'.[17] Men –
predominantly – of their times, like the slide guitarist that
W. C. Handy encountered at the railroad stop in Tutwiler,
caught up in the possibilities of travel offered by trains in
particular. These were people who had 'obviously exploited
the enormous empire of the railroad'.[18]

The lure of travel infuses the sound of the blues, too. And
while movement was expressed in many ways, and could be
found by various means (riding on a pony, in a car, hitchhiking
on the road), the railroad would become a specific image and
sound in the blues – instruments like harmonica, slide guitar
and even the voice (in Howlin' Wolf's 'Smokestack Lightning',
for instance) could mimic the whistle of a passing freighter,
perhaps in celebration of its promise of 'change, transcendence,
and the possibilities of beginning again', and so appealed to
those wandering spirits.[19] Travel – movement and restlessness –

thus became one of the primary themes of the songs of blues musicians, both then and now:

> 'I got to keep moving . . .', 'I got rambling, rambling all on my mind', 'I'm here today and tomorrow I may be gone'. In this respect the bluesman reflected a tendency to be found in American society at large and in black society in particular, where, especially since Emancipation, movement had symbolized freedom . . . Trapped into a kind of economic servitude by sharecropping, with few opportunities to break out of those limitations, travel could itself be an assertion of independence.[20]

And travel they did, most often to the plantations or lumber camps and levees dotted around the South, where the blues found its 'spawning grounds', right in the midst of the dashed hopes of a better life that had been surrendered to 'intolerable living and working conditions'.[21] And for those who would not be able to hitch a ride to some – even temporarily – better place, it was a desire that remained and welled up in song, as John and Alan Lomax discovered when they recorded a chain gang on Parchman Farm singing 'Prettiest Train':

> Prettiest train that I ever seen, man.
> Prettiest train, my Lawd, I ever seen,
> Prettiest train, Lawd, ever seen,
> I 'clare, she run down to Jackson, back to New Orleans,
> New Orleans, a-New Orleans.
> I swear she ran down to Jackson,
> Back to New Orleans.[22]

What is notable about many of the songs that reveal the road to be a state of mind, is that they retain their hold on the imagination of the contemporary listener precisely because they touch upon universal themes – of loss and discovery, of the quasi-spiritual quest (and its dead ends). The life of the wandering blues singer was opened to new possibilities by the spread of the railroad. Some say that before the blues was given form – recorded, preserved and thus capable of moving beyond the confines of a merely oral form of communication and transmission – the earlier pre-blues singers (the so-called 'songsters'), whose repertoire was wide-ranging and included white influences and popular songs of the day, existed as the embodiment of the living character of the music of the South.[23] It was only after the music of this region was differentiated by race into 'hillbilly' (or country) and blues that it became a form that was transmissible beyond its own land and its own culture. Prior to this, it can best be seen in the example of someone like the Texan singer 'Ragtime' Henry Thomas (also known as Ragtime Texas), one of those labelled a 'songster', whose recordings in the first wave of the pre-war blues era (in 1927–9 – the first blues recordings date from around 1920) are slightly misleading, because the date on which they were recorded tends to obscure the fact that the music that made up Thomas's repertoire was probably a reflection of something far older. It included 'snippets from dozens of songs known elsewhere, bits of work and prison camp songs, music taken from country dances, religious songs, the music played by countless similar white musicians', and so on.[24] Thomas, born in the 1870s, was said to be perhaps the oldest of the so-called songsters first recorded in the 1920s, and was – like the singers of the Delta – preoccupied with life on the road, and enamoured of the romance of the railroads, as a listen to the relish with which he hollers and whoops his way through the stops on the way to Kansas City, St Louis and Chicago and back to Texas on the song 'Railroadin' Some' reveals:

Change cars on the TP! [Texas and Pacific Railroad] / Leaving
Fort Worth! Going Through Dallas! Hello, Terrell! Grand Saline!
Silver Lake! Minola! Tyler! Longview! Jefferson! Marshall! Little
Sandy! Big Sandy! And double back to Fort Worth![25]

These recordings are, in the words of one commentator, 'about
the most evocative recordings of their period – a virtual palimpsest
of black vernacular music of the late 19th and early 20th century'.
Henry Thomas, an older musician, was remembered – by witnesses
the famous blues hunter Mac McCormick interviewed in the 1950s
– as a wanderer and itinerant. He played guitar and quills (or 'pan
pipes') made from cane pulled from a riverbed, and was one of
many seemingly hobo musicians who would hang around at every
stop, according to testimonies given to McCormick describing
'dozens of men who used to hang around the domino parlour or
some across-the-tracks tavern until train time when, with everyone
else in town, they'd come over to the depot'.[26] Others who never
made it onto record would be equally willing to celebrate and
serenade the trains that passed through the Delta. H. C. Speir, the
man who recorded Charley Patton, had tried to persuade an old
woman, a 'train caller' at Meridian, who would sing out the stops
ahead. 'I'd have put a harmonica or something like that behind her
. . . but she wouldn't do it.'[27]

The blues developed, in part, from lives that were lived on
the outside or on the margins of society, and in their bringing
together of 'personal sentiments and collective memory' were
mindful of present concerns, while 'framed on the folklore of
the past'.[28] What Lawrence Levine terms the 'central projections
and dreams' of the blues – which is to say the freedom that seemed
off-limits to blacks, and especially Southern blacks living under
Jim Crow laws – were the product of a culture that denied the
kind of expression of selfhood for which the blues would become
a vehicle.[29] There developed, as a result, an attraction to movement

as almost in itself the one avenue towards any kind of self-empowerment available to blacks who were denied economic mobility. And it was pursued self-consciously, argued Levine, as a means of resistance to the fate of life as a wage-slave:

> In 'John Henry' and similar work songs, the request to 'Take my hammer . . . to my captain, / Tell him I'm gone' was accompanied frequently by the admonition: 'If he ask you was I running / Tell him no . . . Tell him I was going across the Blue Ridge Mountains / Walking slow, yes, walking slow.[30]

The travelling Delta blues singers, in particular, have been seen by some as the embodiment of a kind of resistance to the broader culture, and to the conservative elements within their own communities, who regarded their music as 'blasphemous', if not evidence that they were the 'Devil's disciples'. Their attachment to the itinerant life cast them, indeed, as 'proselytizers' of a new secular existence 'in which the belief in freedom became associated with personal mobility – freedom in this world here and now, rather than salvation later on in the next'.[31]

MOVEMENT AND TRANSMISSION

It seems apparent that the repertoire of the early blues singers, which Stephen Calt suggests resulted in the 'wholesale saturation of the South with the same collection of songs', arose from the very centrality of travel and movement to the lives of the musicians.[32] Often they travelled from town to town, and plantation to plantation, bringing entertainment for those who remained more or less confined under conditions of economic need, and inspiring new singers to take up the blues. It is a sound whose essence was distilled through the sharing of ideas, songs and guitar techniques; through what has been termed 'a process of group creation':

The gathering of these many musicians in the Delta was part of the wave of migration bringing blacks to the area as tenant farmers and sharecroppers. Men like [Charley] Patton were perhaps master musicians in the community, but they were not committed professionals. Some musicians would come just for the harvest, others would stay, but all were part of the generally fluctuating community.[33]

As the musicians travelled, so did songs and parts of songs that became part of a common stock of images and floating verses that reappear in slightly altered form in recordings that nonetheless became associated with the 'voice' – the particular *truth* – of certain singers. In other words, despite the common root of many of the images and scenarios of Delta blues, they nonetheless reflected the experience of the individual singer. Charley Patton, John Fahey observes, was like 'an impressionistic painter' who assimilated or came up with lyrical imagery, which often echoed something else he had heard from the 'endless stream of blues verses' he was in touch with.[34]

The figure of the blues singer as one who arrives from some other place offering up music to congregated workers, was a means through which the music that became the blues was established in Mississippi and elsewhere in the South. Looking back to the interest shown in slave songs in the nineteenth century, Samuel Charters wrote that the early influences on the development of the blues encompassed not only 'the rich musical traditions of Africa', but also the songs that itinerant Christian preachers touring the plantations and settlements would teach during church services, which would find their way into the new music, and 'the Scotch and Irish airs' that masters and overseers would whistle in the fields.[35]

W. C. Handy's fortuitous meeting with what we now know as the Delta blues in Tutwiler was to provide the first awareness of a

Alan Lomax and Jerome Weisner of the Archive of American Folk Song – with their 'mobile recording laboratory' – talking outside the Library of Congress, Washington, DC, 1941.

strange and sometimes archaic, otherworldly music that was able to communicate its existence to the outside world. Soon the music would be found by successive waves of 'song hunters' on their own road trips from the north. The father-and-son team of John and Alan Lomax had undertaken the earliest, and most famous, of these expeditionary outings. In 1933 they were touring the South with a portable recording machine fitted into the trunk of a car in search of folk songs for a book that had been commissioned by the Macmillan publishing company (and which would be published in 1934 as *American Ballads and Folk Songs*).[36]

The trip had also been additionally supported by a gift of travel funds from the American Council of Learner Societies and the Library of Congress's Archive of American Folk Song. One aim of scouring the South was to uncover American folk traditions that were not only alive, but quite distinct from any overt connection to the British Isles – then widely believed to be the source of folk song among scholars. Their main discovery was a prisoner in Parchman Farm, Leadbelly (Huddie Ledbetter), whose repertoire of American folk and blues songs they considered to be as close to 'rooted in the precommercial past' as they were likely to find.[37] Due to his incarceration and effective segregation from the outside world, they believed that Leadbelly had remained largely immune to the growing influence of recorded music, the radio and the sophisticated outlook of black jazz musicians; all of which, they thought, were diluting the cultural purity of black folk culture. It was this that they sought to avoid in their attempt to show the scope and breadth of real African American folk music, as Alan Lomax wrote in an appeal for funds from the Carnegie Foundation:

> We propose to go where these influences are not yet dominant: where Negroes are almost entirely isolated from the whites, dependent upon the resources of their own group for amusement: where they are not only preserving a great

body of traditional songs but are also creating new songs in the same idiom.[38]

What they found often struck them as being far more uncanny and altogether weirder, more primitive, and with the power to move the imagination in ways that were unexpected. In his correspondence from their field trips, John Lomax wrote of encountering one singer who momentarily carried him off into thoughts of 'turgid, slow moving rivers in African jungles'.[39]

The Lomaxes were among the earliest intermediaries who would shape the understanding of the blues – or, more broadly, what they referred to as American Folk music – and how it was seen in their own time and by the generations they inspired by their example. In fact, our view of the Delta blues (for better or worse) is cut through with myths and legends, with rumour and half-truth, and is almost defined by its elusiveness.

This, of course, has been much to the dismay of the generations of scholars who scoured the South in search of evidence, and who had made it their life's work to attempt to recover as much factual information about the creators of this music as possible, as well as to more recent scholars, often academic, who are keen on debunking the myths.[40] Their aim has been, most often, to set the record straight and provide as accurate a picture as possible of the life and times of the people and places that spawned this culture – that produced a style of blues music so singular that its reach and influence seemed to become more potent as the decades passed and the further from its source it travelled. This is music that has reached far beyond the geographical confines that originally identified it as music of the South – as blues music; yet not the same blues as that found in New Orleans or Kansas City. But it is in its travel and transmission over time and space that the perceptions of generations of listeners were formed by something other than the kind of truth that comes from factual knowledge. Music is born of particular times and places, to be sure, but it is also a free-floating medium, an itinerant form that is – so to speak – blown, or transported, into alien contexts where it takes on new and unforeseen characteristics; perhaps in the playfulness of new musicians who encounter it and transform it, or in the minds of listeners who allow it to colour their views of their own lives and their own world.

Indeed, the mere observation that this music itself undergoes a journey from its roots is perhaps enough to account for the way in which it becomes a shape-shifting phenomenon intent on recovering its own originary mystery in the minds of new listeners, as it does to history and truth and the pedantic, empirical, probing of the academic mind. The impulse to pursue the factual truth is an understandable one, but one that also tends to sidestep the fact that what came to be *influential* about the Delta blues was the future it had beyond its own time, and the forms its influence took. This is all intimately related to the mystery of it, and to the appeal of the many myths and legends that surround key performers in the development of the music. And this has much to do, arguably, with the fact that its influence was felt most powerfully by a generation of largely white rock musicians for whom it was, by definition, something alien and enigmatic that took them – just as it had done with John and Alan Lomax – far from the concerns of the world they lived in and into a new imaginary space of heightened aesthetic experience.

Even the snippets of factual information and the fragments of visual traces of long-vanished performers that *did* surface seemed to do little to confound the music's aura of strangeness. Its otherworldliness is not merely found in its strangeness, but in the fact that it more often than not came from a culture still characterized by folk forms and old ways, and where written and documentary forms were not yet an essential part of the arts of preservation and transmission that saw the music spread across

the Delta. When Alan Lomax, in 1942, presented to the Library of
Congress his 'List of American Folk Songs on Commercial Records'
– which was essentially a research document – he prefaced the
document by noting the labours involved in its creation. It was
based, he wrote, on auditing and listening to some 'three thousand
odd commercial records' in order that his knowledge might allow
'the interested musician or student of American society to explore
this unknown body of Americana with readiness'. Yet the time
involved in reviewing all the material, when combined with his
first-hand knowledge of the music of the South, left him feeling
that something much larger had been lost. 'I feel sure that I have
heard only a quarter of the interesting records', he noted:

> for example, I was able nowhere to find a large group of Okehs
> or Gennetts [popular record labels of the day] to audition . . .
> It seems to be impossible in the present state of confusion that
> exists in the files of commercial recording companies to say
> which records are in print and which are not.[41]

And so, when the most basic evidence of the music does not exist,
and its makers have passed on or grown old and forgetful, it is
little wonder that those scratchy old 78 records became more
mysterious: more answers were sought, but while the questions
multiplied, the past – most often – remained elusive.

It is such gaps in knowledge that have ensured that many
of the performers associated with the Delta blues, in particular,
would be shrouded in myths and legends. What remained of so
many who did not live to see their recordings recognized by later
generations was the ghostly trace of the phonograph records
along with whatever other information could be unearthed from
a time when so much of life was undocumented, or not preserved
for posterity.

3 ROBERT JOHNSON'S CROSSROADS

It's hard to imagine sharecroppers or plantation field
hands at hop joints, relating to songs like these. You have
to wonder if Johnson was playing for an audience that
only he could see, off in the future. 'The stuff I got'll bust
your brains out,' he sings. Johnson is serious, like the
scorched earth.

Bob Dylan, *Chronicles: Volume One* (2004)

THE FAUSTIAN PACT

Robert Johnson was among the last of the significant country
blues singers who could trace a direct personal connection to the
previous generation, and is, in some respects, the last in that line
of loner itinerant types who travelled the Delta and farther afield,
before it was overtaken by the new electric blues that the migrants
from the Delta would make in Chicago. Although he died in 1938,
he was indirectly responsible for the discovery of the singer who
would carry the Delta blues into new territory, in both the
geographical and musical senses of the word.

When Alan Lomax went to the Delta looking for Robert
Johnson in 1941, only to discover that he was dead, he was instead
sent in the direction of a young singer, McKinley Morganfield,
who went by the name of Muddy Waters and was working on
the large Stovall Farms near Clarksdale, driving a tractor – and
selling bootleg whiskey on the side just to make some extra
money. Waters initially thought that Lomax was some kind of
undercover cop or Federal agent who had rumbled the secret
operation: 'I couldn't figure it out . . . I didn't know whether he
was one of them smart police coming after me, or what the heck
was going on.'[1] Lomax's discovery would become central to the

subsequent rediscovery of the blues in the 1950s and '60s, and a living link between the Delta blues and its offshoots in rock music (Waters appeared, as a sort of elder statesmen of American music, alongside Bob Dylan, Eric Clapton, Van Morrison and others, in The Band's celebrated concert movie *The Last Waltz*, filmed in 1976 and released two years later).

Johnson's recordings, however, would be an even more direct link to the rock music of the 1960s that revived interest in the – by then – almost forgotten blues of the Delta; this was even though he had been preceded as a recording artist by many others whose popularity in their lifetimes made them still widely known and remembered decades later. Johnson, by contrast, was a fairly obscure and minor recording artist while he was alive.

As a teenager in the late 1920s, Johnson had been known to Son House and Willie Brown, both close associates of Charley Patton. He would hang around in the clubs where the older men played, looking for guitar lessons. The story told by Son House was that while the young Johnson had shown significant talent as a harmonica player, he was hopeless as a blues guitarist. After receiving little encouragement from his would-be mentors – they were said to have indulged him up to a point, allowing him to take up their guitars when they were between sets – he disappeared, only to return about a year later all of a sudden endowed with a sophisticated facility on the guitar, and by the standards of some of the other Delta players – such as Son House, who roughly manhandled his instrument, wringing and bashing out sound – he appeared to have come out of nowhere. The fact that he was able to play so well was the cause of speculation then, and the kind of mystery that – in time – fed into his legend. How else could a young man's fortunes be so turned around, the logic ran, unless he had found some shortcut to the kind of accomplishment that elevated him above peers and predecessors? Yet at the same time Son House, who swung between the church and the blues, may have sensed something of the 'demonic' about the young man – 'he had a cataract in one eye; he often played with his back to other musicians, which some of them took as proof that he had something to hide . . . and he favored unusual guitar tunings' that may have been suspected, according to the folk beliefs of the day, as the result of a retuning job done at the crossroads.[2] The truth seemed to be more mundane: Johnson had apprenticed himself to an older guitarist, Ike Zinermon, and spent considerable time travelling to 'juke joints and work camps' in the Hazelhurst and Crystal Springs area in the south of Mississippi. Given Johnson's association with the crossroads myth, it seems apt that the man who reputedly transformed his guitar playing, Zinermon, 'claimed that he [Zinermon] had learned guitar while practicing in a graveyard at midnight, sitting on top of tombstones'.[3] Perhaps he passed on some of the sense of the demonic that others clearly perceived in Robert Johnson.

More than any other blues singer from the Delta tradition, Johnson has been the subject of the most persistent and fanciful stories; a figure 'mythologized' by romantics, who seemed only too willing to buy into the story of how he 'went to the crossroads and negotiated an unholy bargain with the Devil'.[4] But as easy as it may be to see these stories for what they are today – exaggerations, the conflation of song lyrics with biography, outright fantasy – it is, in truth, easy to be sceptical now, some 50-odd years after the release of the first reissue on an LP album of Johnson's 1930s recordings, *King of the Delta Blues Singers* (released by Columbia in 1961). It is also important to remember that not only had some of the many gaps in Johnson's life been filled in, but there also emerged an understanding of how the life and times of someone in his position should be seen in the light of what is known about the prevalence of supernatural beliefs among African Americans living in the South at that time.

But, as Martin Scorsese, director of the film *Feel Like Going Home* (2003) – a film partly about Johnson and one of seven documentaries by Scorsese entitled *The Blues* – was keen to point out, for those who first heard Johnson's music on those early reissues, this was someone who existed as 'pure myth'. There could be no other way of comprehending him, so out of reach of the present were the facts behind the sound and the voice on that record, and so unencumbered by a single frame of photographic proof that he actually existed (the two photographs that are now known would not be uncovered until the 1970s, and not published for another decade following that). Any attempt to look at how travelling and movement become written into the history of twentieth-century American music cannot sidestep the Johnson myth. The images his music has called up for listeners – of unrelenting torment, the presence of bad spirits and the oppression of nameless 'blues' that fall like hail – has seemed to reveal that many of his songs relate the life of the road to the most essential truths about human experience: the purpose of life, the inevitability of death and so on. The Faustian pact that became one source of the fascination with which his music was perceived, became difficult to separate from a 'music of almost supernatural power and presence', which had 'an undercurrent of impending doom'.[5]

'Cross Road Blues', from a post-1960s perspective slanted by the form of presentation that was then common among 'confessional' singer-songwriters – in the stripped down voice, and with a lone guitar as some kind of guarantor of realism – might easily be seen in both biographical and metaphorical terms. In terms of the former, it was undoubtedly a song that showed 'in actual and poetic terms a consciously considered nomadic life':[6]

Standin' at the crossroad
I tried to flag a ride

Robert Johnson, the other 'King of the Delta Blues Singers', whose songs seemed to lay bare the travails of a 'tormented drifter'.

Didn't nobody seem to know me
everybody pass me by

Such might have been the experience of many blues singers of
the 1920s and '30s who hitched on the highway. But compared
to descriptions of the mere practicalities of making a living, the
subject caught out on the road in this crossroad seems to be aware
that there is some risk involved in being alone and on the road at
that precise location when darkness falls:

Mmm, the sun goin' down, boy
dark gon' catch me here
oooo ooee eeee

And, finally, in despair, calling out for a friend:

You can run, you can run
tell my friend-boy Willie Brown
Lord, that I'm standin' at the crossroad, babe
I believe I'm sinkin' down.

It is the foreboding nature of a scenario situated in such a
place at that time of night with the subject apparently helpless
to escape – on his knees, pleading for God's mercy, but ultimately
'sinkin' down', being pulled under – that helps to evoke the
unstated 'Devil's bargain' that is implicit in the lyric. Yet at the
same time there is a way of looking at it that is not so overloaded
with this symbolism; that is to say, it reflects, no less, a universal
theme, drawing on the much more common 'dilemma of choice'
that anyone who had been, metaphorically speaking, at some
'crossroads' or another in their life, would understand.[7] Making
a 'deal with the Devil', from that point of view, is a way of
dramatizing a choice to follow one of two paths that are defined

by uncertainty, if not the power to direct one's own future. And perhaps it is the choice that Johnson, like many other musicians, made; to set aside the normal kind of family life known by those who live settled lives, and opt for something other than what was considered the Christian life.

What makes it, metaphorically, a choice that sides with 'the Devil' is just that – viewed in historical context – this was a way of life that was characterized by rootlessness and vice, by the breaking of community standards, and which additionally carried blues singers into all sorts of trouble because, in their apparent willingness to go their own way, they raised the suspicion of white society. And, as Adam Gussow argues, in blues song there is a common theme of romantic abandonment or 'lonesomeness' that draws on the likely travails of being out there on the road, alone, in a world where the colour of your skin marked you out and, as a travelling musician, made you conspicuously different.[8]

But, on the other hand, the symbolism of the crossroads that Johnson was drawing on went very much deeper into African American folk beliefs that were still common in the South, and that seemed to easily suggest themselves to those who encountered the blues and may, Robert Palmer argued, have even been 'calculated from the very beginning' by blues performers to 'play into the beliefs and fears of their audiences in the joints'.[9] It was a kind of 'image-making' that helped to sell records.[10] The religious-supernatural beliefs that went by the names hoodoo, voodoo and conjure are prevalent as subject-matter in many blues songs – 'Got My Mojo Working' (Muddy Waters), 'Hoodoo Lady' (Memphis Minnie), 'Hoodoo Hoodoo' (Sonny Boy Williamson), 'Low Down Mojo Blues' (Blind Lemon Jefferson), to name a few.[11]

But for some listeners, the spectre of the supernatural was also present in songs with no explicit reference to the casting of spells or conjuring practices. Alan Lomax, in his review of American Folk Songs for the Library of Congress, chose several of Robert

View of a country road, Mississippi Delta, 1937. Robert Johnson, during his travels, would have walked many similar routes.

Johnson's most well-known 78s: 'Cross Road Blues' was one – the others were 'Hell Hound on My Trail' and 'Stones in My Passway'. Alone among the 500 or so songs listed in the document, all of which receive very brief descriptions as to their musical style and lyrical content, Johnson's songs seemed to have stood out to him as particular instances of the influence of superstitious beliefs, and all are accompanied by the remark, 'traces of voodoo'.[12]

THE DEVIL IS ON THE ROAD

The proximity of New Orleans, which was within easy reach of the Delta, has been seen as an explanation for the prevalence of these supernatural references in Delta blues songs. In *Flash of the Spirit*, Robert Farris Thompson suggests that 'the blues of the Mississippi Delta' draw on those West African beliefs and traditions found also in New Orleans, and 'sometimes make cryptic reference to Kongo-influenced charms'.[13] Some of the basic elements are expressed in Muddy Waters's song 'Hoochie Coochie Man', which details some of the paraphernalia the conjurer or hoodoo practitioner might employ to turn events one way or another – black cat bones, mojo hands and other fetishes employed to cast a spell on some unwitting target; in this case, a pretty woman.

Newbell Niles Puckett, in an exhaustive treatise titled *Folk Beliefs of the Southern Negro*, published in 1926, reveals a number of texts dating back to the previous century that supply African American variations on what Europeans would identify as the Faust legend. These are in the form of instructions that reveal the means through which one's desires might be revealed. To attain musical mastery of stringed instruments such as the banjo, violin or guitar, one might best guarantee this by learning from the master conjurer – 'the Devil' – himself. 'If you want to make a contract with the Devil', Puckett was advised by a New Orleans conjurer, it was necessary to be prepared. 'First trim your finger nails as close as you possibly can', he was told:

> Take a black cat bone and a guitar and go to a lonely fork in the roads at midnight. Sit down there and play your best piece, thinking of and wishing for the devil all the while . . . After a time you will feel something tugging at your instrument . . . Then the devil will hand you his instrument to play and will

accompany you on yours. After doing this for a time he will seize your fingers and trim the nails until they bleed, finally taking his guitar back and returning your own. Keep on playing; do not look around. His music will become fainter and fainter as he moves away . . . You will be able to play any piece you desire on the guitar and you can do anything you want to in the world, but you have sold your eternal soul to the devil and are his in the world to come.[14]

Stanley Booth's story 'Standing at the Crossroads' (1991) seems, on first reading, a fantastic debunking of the myth of the bluesman (Robert Johnson, in this case) selling his soul to the Devil at some country crossroad, but it restates, in humorous form, those beliefs just outlined. An 'Old Black Man', who we learn is named Cyclone, arrives in some remote woods after escaping what seems like a lynch mob – tarred and feathered, and with his shoes removed by his assailants to prevent him from escaping, he nonetheless slipped free. The attempt to inhibit him from running by taking his shoes, he remarks, was a miscalculation: 'dey wahnt doin' nothin' but givin' me a head start'.[15]

As the old man sits down to nurse his aching feet and check the contents of the luggage – a guitar case – that he has hauled along on his escape, we get the sense that if he is not exactly the Devil, then he is at least some kind of conjurer who perhaps just likes to *pretend* he's everything that anyone who meets him *thinks* he is. He tips out the contents of the guitar case, checking for damage and taking an inventory of goods, occasionally commenting on their condition:

Lodestone. Madstone, Devil's snuff. *Ruint.* (Dumps it out) Devil's Shoestrings. Wet as a Rat. Dragon Blood powder. Maybe I can dry it out. Black cat bone. Be Together powder. Dragon Blood Stick. Black cat ashes. Love Me powder. Five

Finger grass. Asafidity. (Sniffs) *Phew.* Rattlesnake dust. (Shakes his head.) John the Conqueror root. Wonder of the World root. Mojo hands. Tobys. Cunyun jacks. Graveyard dirt . . . Mercy, mercy. (Looks around, becomes solemn) Down in de *low*-ground, barefoot as a *yard*-dog, lost as a *by*-God.[16]

As Stanley Booth tells it, Robert Johnson – in flight from a jealous husband – encounters this figure in woods near a crossroad, and is at first startled to see what he takes to be a barefoot traveller. The old man, Cyclone, expresses his admiration for Johnson's *shoes*, although in a manner that is subtle enough to trick the young man, and informs him that while it is easy to become fixated on the supposed comforts of shoes, in the end they bring only misery:

> OLD BLACK MAN: Never wear shoes. Shoes tilt de spine and
> alter de constituent of de human brain. Black *and* White.
> I done studied it. Worked for years with a doctor, white
> man, medical doctor. Fack, me an' him just parted.
> YOUNG BLACK MAN (coming closer): You a musicianer?
> OLD BLACK MAN: Musicianer, root doctor, rain maker, water
> witch, card dealer, crap shooter, spiritual adviser. I am
> de seventh son of de seventh daughter of a seventh son.[17]

Cyclone introduces himself, but Johnson figures this must be the man he has been told so much about – that he has been looking for – and asks him how he might be able to improve his playing on the guitar he is carrying with him. The old man takes his guitar and retunes it and plays a song – 'This song spoze to be in Spanish [tuning], and I b'lieve you in Mexican.' Then the old man gets up to perform a trick out on the crossroad, asking Johnson to remove his shoes or else it will fail:

A plantation store, Lake Charles, Mississippi Delta, July 1936.

CYCLONE: Walk to de center of de crossroads. (Cyclone goes
along, keeping his distance.) Close yo' eyes. Turn around
three times to de lef'. Now three times to de right. Keep
yo' eyes shot. Now step out of yo' shoes.

ROBERT: My shoes?

CYCLONE: Hush yo' mouf, boy. Dis de mos' important part.
Step backwards out yo' shoes. Now open yo' eyes.

Cyclone then instructs Robert to drink an entire bottle of 'Dr Whitlow's Tonic', a remedy he had been carrying along with all the other charms, and which will send the one who consumes it to sleep. 'And when you wake up', he says, 'this will all be like a dream. You will be able to learn anything you want to play on the guitar, and yo' shoes will be waitin' for you in Hell.'[18]

The Johnson myth, then, reflects the superstitions that surrounded the life of the wandering musician: it is on the road that one encounters conjurers and tricksters, and it was on the road that Johnson lived his short adult life. Throughout the Delta, and up into Tennessee – just as he sang in 'Traveling Riverside Blues' – he had a network of women and family members who looked after him when he was on the move. 'His life was divided into any number of networks or compartments', the researcher Mack McCormick recalled.[19] And he travelled under a number of aliases – Robert Sax, Robert Spenser – that came in useful if there was trouble when he was around, as they might ease his passage and avoid him being blamed for things he didn't do, which was sometimes a risk when blowing in and out of strange towns.[20] It seems, too, that all of the contacts he had who would provide him with a temporary place to stay were unaware of each other. 'Throughout all of them he moved as a solitary figure, cryptic, guarded, somewhat secretive', McCormick said:

> He didn't like to play with anyone else much, and no one who travelled with him ever considered himself a partner. He was well-mannered, he was soft-spoken, he was indecipherable. No one seems to have any idea where the music came from.[21]

The themes in the songs sung by Johnson are weighty – transcendental, mythic, concerned with exile as the permanent human condition – and seem to relate the experience of brutally hard lives in a language and imagery that is cloaked in an almost biblical view of the land, and of human fate within it. 'The rambling figure depicted in his songs', Ted Gioia argues, 'was no invention on Johnson's part, but an accurate reflection' of the life he led.[22] That life was, most of the time, a kind of near vagabond existence, but one that encompassed a fair degree of locational variety, compared to some singers who had spent much of their performing days in and around the Mississippi Delta. Charley Patton's 'main "beat" was in the northwestern quarter of Mississippi', for instance (although he played elsewhere).[23] Johnson performed as far north as Canada and New Jersey – where he played Italian songs at a local wedding – and travelled to Texas to record all his sides. He was always ready, his sometime travelling companion Johnny Shines said, to hop on a train at short notice.

As many scholars and researchers have noted, the association of Johnson with the legend of the crossroads, as a doom-laden figure, presents an alluring and romanticized ideal of the Delta bluesman that tends to overpower some of the more mundane details about how he earned a living, including the variety of music he might have had to play beyond the few dozen recordings he left behind. If the evidence of the surges in popularity that Robert Johnson's music has enjoyed is anything to go by – including a million-selling 1990s release that won a Grammy – the romantic version of his life continues to exercise a hold over people. The entire Johnson myth is simply such a powerful force in connecting the contemporary listener to something that remains essentially mysterious about an individual, and so beyond our grasp.[24] But Johnson, the travelling singer to top them all, who could apparently dip into many styles and enjoyed playing the pop hits of the day, while also being the voice of those timeless mid-1930s recordings, must be seen as a figure who existed at another crossroads: the crossroads where the more or less anonymous performer becomes an artist, and where rural life gives way to modernity.

Johnson provides, Paul Gilroy argues, 'one axis of [Jimi] Hendrix's world by marking the historical transition of everyday blues into the altered tempos of the industrial age':

> That fatal crossroads is only one of a number of special sites where tradition and modernity intersect, or, more accurately, where two discrepant modernities – one of the plantation and the other of the metropolis – came into exhilarating and troubling contact.[25]

But blues purists sometimes tend to take a different view: for them, Robert Johnson, a late figure in the chronology of Delta blues – but one whose name now looms large in its history due to his influence on white musicians – was not that 'original', they argue; in terms of popularity among black audiences in the 1930s, he was a 'nonentity' who, unlike other blues artists, arguably did not redefine the terms of his genre within his own lifetime.[26]

ROBERT JOHNSON INVENTS HIMSELF

Recording and having a presence on record – regardless of how successful the records actually were – was undoubtedly a sign of arrival, which probably justified their choice to follow an itinerant lifestyle marked by uncertainty. In time, after these records resurfaced, the artists behind them became representative of a certain kind of integrity that seemed to go along with their uncompromising attitude to life, at a time when most African Americans were still forced to live within a profoundly unequal society. Yet it seems equally likely that the record companies of the 1920s and '30s shaped the perception of the Delta bluesman as a lone drifter, flirting with danger and singing of his experience – and often, indeed, dying due to the vicissitudes of a life on the road (as was the case with Robert Johnson, who was reputedly murdered after a performance, and Blind Lemon Jefferson, who was caught out in a snowstorm and froze to death).

Their recordings were also brought into existence through a process that drew in various intermediaries – from talent scouts to record company producers. H. C. Speir, who acted on behalf of some of the major record companies, for instance, only made test recordings of those singers who were able to come up with at least four original songs – a clear move in the direction of cultivating the singer as considered artist and away from 'what was expected of musicians in clubs or dances', where it seems to have been common for the repertoire to be varied enough to incorporate pop hits of the day.[27] In a somewhat revisionist recent history, Elijah Wald even goes as far as to argue that 'the songs blues musicians played in the studio not only failed to represent their day-to-day repertoires, but were often created specifically for the recording session' and never played again.[28] The association between the singer, expressing a more or less unique individuality on record, and the songs that they claimed as their own, was a lot more tenuous than in later decades, when mass media – especially television – made the singers the visually recognizable personality behind songs that, in the case of later rock music in particular, are elevated above the ordinary only because they bear the stamp of individuality. In fact, it was also true – unsurprisingly, given the lack of visual exposure of these musicians – that the artists behind some of the records that were in circulation would likely have been unknown even to those who might have had some familiarity with their songs. It is a point illustrated in the reminiscence of David 'Honeyboy' Edwards, who recounted once coming across Robert Johnson, his sometime travelling companion, who was playing on a street corner in Greenwood, Mississippi, and had become involved in an argument with a passer-by about one of his own songs:

The Gunter Hotel, San Antonio, Texas. Room 414 was the location of Robert Johnson's first recording sessions in November 1936.

He was standing there on the street, and this lady walked up to him and said, 'Can you play "Terraplane Blues"?' 'Cause that record had just come out, but she didn't know who she was talkin' to. He said, 'Miss, that's my number.' . . . She said, 'I don't believe you.' He said, 'Give me fifteen cents and I'll play it.'[29]

It is easy enough to find ways to downplay Johnson's significance – there's the fact that he copped most of his trademark licks, lyrical imagery and mode of expression from what had come before, and from having watched and observed contemporaries or listened closely to their records.[30] There is an undeniable truth in this, but at the same time, seeing Johnson merely as the sum of these parts, taken and simply cobbled into the body of work we know today, is to downplay what is truly significant about him. This is the sense that he really does act as the bridge to other destinations that these Delta blues have followed: the post-war electric blues of Muddy Waters, Elmore James and others in Chicago, and also the 1960s and '70s rock music (of The Rolling Stones, Led Zeppelin and so on) that was largely a British creation. There might be historical luck in the timing of Johnson's appearance as a recording artist, able to develop something new out of the old; but there is no accident in the influence. It is *that* 'voice' that appeals because it rises above the obvious influences. It is whatever there is in that sound – to which we apply the terms 'real' and 'authentic' – that endures.

Johnson is arguably the first truly modern blues singer – simply because his self-invention was so obvious and so self-conscious. His distance from the oral tradition that spawned early Delta predecessors is evident in the fact that he learned from their records; but it is also there in the 'singular vision', the 'emotional directness' in those recordings that 'cuts to the quick'.[31] In terms of the blues that preceded him, what Johnson did more than anyone else, Ted Gioia argues, was 'to bring together the different strands of the American blues tradition into a holistic style'.[32] And it is a style that expands – both vocally and instrumentally – the parameters of his blues predecessors which, Gioia argues, he 'had worked so relentlessly' at, as he probably sought to 'surpass the competing guitarists of his time and place' and seal his reputation:[33]

Johnson has an almost endless number of guitar tricks
at his disposal: churning boogie rhythms, dancing triplets,
syncopated turnarounds, masterful slide phrases, ingenious
counterpoint lines, fidgety vamps, tasty instrumental breaks
and interludes, dramatic changes in tone and texture. His
vocals are, if anything, even more wide-ranging.[34]

As we have seen, Lawrence Levine suggests that many
examples of Delta blues express nothing so much as a sense
of 'pure self'.[35] For instance, it seems to be overwhelmingly the
case that most Delta blues are sung in the first person and contain
heavy hints that the lyrical content is, if not directly biographical,
reflective of the experience of the singer. Yet this idea that the
songs are a direct route to something essential, some pure state
of being, might – for those with a more sceptical outlook – be
complicated by the question of the originality of song composition
which hangs over recordings that display echoes of earlier records.
The sources of Robert Johnson's songs have been found in
numerous other records, and many by singers from outside the
Delta. While the influence of Son House and Willie Brown on
Johnson was first-hand and occurred at a formative period in his
development, their influence 'was outweighed by the recordings'
of figures such as Peetie Wheatstraw (from Tennessee) on some
of Johnson's vocal mannerisms, and Kokomo Arnold (from
Georgia) on his slide guitar playing and on song themes, and
'elsewhere we can detect the influence of Leroy Carr, Lonnie
Johnson, and other successful recording artists of the era'.[36]

Because many blues songs became fairly widely known
through record releases, the later performers, like Robert
Johnson, might copy what they had heard, but – crucially – the
fact that their recordings would be available for others to hear
as well, showing up any obvious borrowings, meant that they
probably also felt compelled to introduce elements of novelty

and originality. In fact, it could have been that 'later blues musicians were less free' to use, for instance, 'formulaic phrases as elements of a common vocabulary' because they would have been so easily identified with any well-known records that were then in circulation. It meant that 'instead of simply using a formulaic lick or metaphor', the player had to:

> either quote its canonic form or consciously vary it. Depending on who was doing it, that kind of conscious variation kept the blues straining in two opposite directions, towards high art and towards kitsch.[37]

And all the while, ever since records began to circulate widely in the early 1920s, blues singers had borrowed and adapted existing songs, using numerous examples of what David Evans, in *Big Road Blues*, refers to as the common 'processes' for improvising on existing songs (which range from localizing lyrics to changing instrumentation to garbling the words).[38] As an early blues scholar, Max Jones, argued in an analysis of blues song written in the 1940s, 'enterprising singers' used 'odds and ends' that circulated among the community of players and singers, and which ensured that the blues was 'part-created *in the performance* from scraps of verse and melody known to the community as a whole'.[39] The question of originality and authorship was a moot point – because the remade songs were given back 'with new, and often topical flavouring'.[40] And we might see the same issue arise if we look further back, in the way that even a seminal figure like Charley Patton, who it is reasonable to assume was performing before records became a common source of influence, was nonetheless believed to have pulled lines, verses and musical motifs from a common stock of elements that seemed to float freely within the culture, but did so without losing his unique voice.[41] The problem that some blues purists seem to have with

Robert Johnson is that he did not 'give back' in quite the same way – rather, his influence surfaced in remote times and places, and in the form of something that seemed quite distant from the blues; namely, rock music.

The fact that many of Robert Johnson's songs borrowed or developed elements of the form and style of blues that were passed around, shared, and reinterpreted by one singer after another, does not detract from the fact that they reflected something of the common experience of blacks in the American South. It is in this sense that Levine's reference to a purity of experience coming through in the voice should be understood. It is important to make this point because it is 'pure self', or something like it – authenticity; a sense of believability – that ends up transmitting the work of singers like Charley Patton and Robert Johnson across time and space, and allows them to seemingly bridge generational, geographical and racial boundaries. Getting caught up in a kind of empiricism that seeks only to reveal the factual basis of the Delta blues in its time and place may be adhering to some kind of academic standard of how we might recover the past. But in seeking to counter the romantic distortions, it somewhat fails to recognize that recorded music, by its very nature, is something that travels and circulates in ways that break the hold of the past, and not least the networks of transmission common to folk traditions and folk memory. Elijah Wald's *Escaping the Delta* argues that the image we have of the itinerant bluesmen (men like Patton, Tommy Johnson, Robert Johnson and others) is 'unrepresentative' of what *blues* (as if it was one unified form) actually were in the times and places that those singers plied their trade. It may be *our* image of what the blues in the 1920s and '30s were, but it does not, so the argument goes, reflect what the audience for these race records would have, at the time, identified as the blues. The winners, as always, get to rewrite history (or have it rewritten for them). Because Robert Johnson, Wald argues, was not at all popular in his own time, his contemporary place in the history of the blues is a paradox. The simple truth is that his greatest influence (arguably far above other Delta singers) was on a certain kind of rock music. And, whatever way one looks at it, that rock music was a new variant of the blues – in spirit, in thematic concerns and in the development of the blues when severed from its 'folk' roots.

There is luck and timing in the fact that Robert Johnson's influence increased as the decades passed, whereas the influence of his contemporaries waned. The fact that Johnson's recordings appeared in an era – the '60s – when a new youth culture, whose focal point was music, was taking off, meant that the conditions for transmitting the presence that so evidently pervades those recordings were almost perfect. Robert Johnson was also marketed to the '60s generation as something that they would recognize – a singer with a unique 'voice' and body of work, which was in contrast to how previous releases of Delta blues had been presented. They were often compilations of various singers; but the Columbia Records release of *King of the Delta Blues Singers* was the first to feature just one lone singer and one singular artistic vision.

It is the songs he recorded and the quality of those recordings – sourced from original masters – that have ensured he has travelled so well. The obvious comparison is with the much rougher-sounding recordings of Charley Patton, whose legacy was only preserved on old 78 shellac discs which, in spite of the wonders of modern technology, ensured that he remains partially submerged in time; behind the crackles and pops of the source discs.

Although recorded in settings that seem far removed from contemporary hi-tech studios – hotel rooms, an empty warehouse space – these were not field recordings in the style of the Lomaxes with their car-mounted tape machine (which actually captured

The cover of Columbia Records' release of 1969, *King of the Delta Blues Singers, Volume II*. Interior of the hotel room in San Antonio, Texas, November 1936.

performances *in the field*). Johnson was recorded under what were then comparatively modern conditions, with attention paid to factors that might adversely affect the quality of the finished product, and with some novel measures taken to keep the performance on track. As recording engineer Don Law recounted, the second Robert Johnson session in Dallas – in the punishing heat of June 1937 – was complicated by the fact that there was too much noise entering the room from the street. So, despite the rising temperature, they had to seal all the windows and sacrifice whatever air had been coming into the room to get rid of the sound of traffic and people outside. They were forced, Law said, to work 'shirtless' and 'with electric fans blowing across cakes of ice' to make up for the lack of air conditioning – an image quite at odds with the representation of the session on the rear sleeve of the second volume of *King of the Delta Blues Singers,* which shows the producer and engineer fully clothed.[42]

The recording process placed time constraints on the length of songs, for the most part ruling out rambling 'blues' which, in their oral and folkloric form, could be extended as long as the impulse to sing maintained its hold on the player, and the attention of the audience. The Delta blues singers, already cast as loners within their own milieu, were on the cusp of a different world. If the sense of movement and restlessness in these recordings lent them the ability to sing of their experience in a way that rings true today, they were – in their rootless ways – strangely representative of the changing, modernizing world. In developing aspects of their blues that allowed them to stand out and be perceived as unique enough to be recorded, they also reflected the importance that was placed on individual subjectivity in the modern world, and within the conditions of production that characterized record making they would become part of developments that were even more wholly modern. They existed as creators in almost laboratory-like conditions – the experimental space of the recording studio, and the means it used to isolate the musician from producers, such as glass-fronted booths (they were in another room in the case of Johnson's San Antonio recordings) and materials for baffling the sound. Then there were the differences in performance that would shape studio work which, as Evan Eisenberg writes in *The Recording Angel,* were 'strong metaphors for modern life' themselves: 'the abstracted audience; the sense of producing an object and of mass-producing a commodity; the deconstruction of time by takes and its reconstruction by splicing'.[43]

There is no audience in the traditional sense within this kind of context; only potential and anonymous listeners – who might never cross paths with this music. There is, corresponding to this, the 'solitude' of the listener, and the 'collapse of a public architecture of time and the creation of a private interior design of time' contradicts everything that 'music making once seemed to be'.[44] By the late 1960s and '70s, as we will see, many of the musicians of that generation who were inspired by these blues found a way to break out of what they felt to be confining about the laboratory-like conditions of record making.

Whatever the metaphorical hellhounds that dogged Robert Johnson were, the experience of being out there on the move offered the touch of authenticity that the songs of the hard life seemed to require to retain their sense of being undiluted and free from compromise (qualities that were keenly perceived by listeners from the 1950s onwards), and the perception of which has guaranteed their trans-generational appeal. Shortly before his murder Johnson left a handwritten note, whose words now appear on his headstone in Clarksdale, Mississippi: 'Jesus of Nazareth, King of Jerusalem. I know that my Redeemer liveth, and that He will call me from my grave.' Little could he know that his real redeemers did not reside in the transcendental hereafter, but in the seemingly distant culture of white rock music, particularly among the 1960s baby-boomer generation, whose interest in the blues, and in Johnson, was driven by an image of authenticity (in his apparent suffering for his art) and the uncompromising freedom his lifestyle was perceived to embody.

4 JOURNEYS INTO THE FUTURE: FROM BLUES AND ROCK 'N' ROLL TO DYLAN

EASY RIDERS

It is almost impossible to overstate the importance of travel in the development of these blues, because it is music and its influence that travels and continues to pass through transitions even after its original representatives cease to perform. In the American South in the 1920s and '30s, the instruments that helped define the Delta blues, the guitar and harmonica – being both eminently portable and suited to travelling – became the principal means through which the music and its players were able to travel and gain a wider influence than the limited (in most cases) popular appeal through sales or exposure by other means might have allowed.

And while the association of music itself – any kind of music – with travelling was not new, simply because before broadcast media became a dominant force it was how music got around and reached new ears, through the Delta blues it was transformed into something unique to that place, particularly in the period between the two World Wars. Without the need to maintain a band, for instance, it was much cheaper and easier for a lone blues musician to get around. As such, travelling could become a way of life that offered an alternative to the more routine occupations of the day – working in the fields, picking cotton and so on. It is no accident that the blues of that era, from a contemporary perspective, seemed at some point 'to become the property of loners', from places like Mississippi, Texas and Virginia: 'discographical phantoms with guitars for whom the blues wasn't just an approach to music, but a state of mind'.[1] Travelling was simply central to how the music of the Delta, in particular, spread among its musicians in the first place – it was, at some point, a new kind of style to be learned from visiting musicians – and was later taken further afield into new territory that would break it out of what Robert Palmer termed the 'regional straightjacket' of those times and places that gave rise to it, and had defined it as Delta blues.[2]

One important reason that these blues would become known so widely many decades later was that they were recorded at a time when the music industry was going through one of its early booms. The traffic between representatives of the nascent music industry in Memphis, Chicago, Kansas and the Delta was part of the search for new performers to provide songs to sell to the large audiences who purchased what were then known as 'race' records. These were records made by black Americans for, and marketed to, a black audience. The Mississippi Delta, which in historical terms provided a veritable who's who of the blues, was in relatively easy reach of these cities, and Chicago in particular, which just happened to be the second most important centre of the then burgeoning record industry after New York City.

The modernity of the Delta blues is perhaps not the first thing that springs to mind when listening to a scratchy old recording of Charley Patton, but the new medium of 78 records marked a change in how music, in general, was disseminated to far-flung listeners. If we contrast this with the situation some decades before, the means of transmission were somewhat different. In the United States, minstrel revues, carnivals and tent shows had enjoyed widespread popularity since the early nineteenth century, and usually featured musicians of some sort, often alongside numerous other attractions (from bearded ladies and magicians to acrobats and dangerous animals).[3] But the association between travel and music that arises in relation to the Delta blues is different, and becomes more to do with travel as a kind of self-exploration. It should be no surprise, then, that the bluesman's instrument of choice – which was typically a guitar or a harmonica – shares the accolade of being a good travelling companion, a so-called 'easy rider', with the female partners whose often temporary presence in the songster's life can be identified in numerous songs, where they become important subjects, and representative of the pick-up-and-go lifestyle of the travelling musician. These songs usually refer to either finding, losing or travelling with a woman who – as the giver and taker of sexual favours – becomes a central source of blues itself. On the road, however, there is no permanence in relationships, and nothing is more important than the desire to keep on moving, as expressed in songs like 'See See Rider' (aka 'Easy Rider'), a staple for numerous performers since its first recording by Ma Rainey in 1924:

> See see rider
> See what you have done.
> Made me love you,
> Now you done gone.

And so it is that travel offered relief from the blues – in escaping one's woes – but at the same time increased the chances that the restless musician might arrive at new situations and encounters that merely produced further blues. And it is for this reason that the very idea of having *the blues* often implied being on the move, on the run or of existing in the expectation that some kind of change might help to temporarily dispel the burden that was weighing one down. The encounters that helped shape the blues within the Delta took place in particular locations where there was a lot of musical activity and interchange: for instance, around the Dockery Plantation and through the influence of Charley Patton in the 1920s, and in Helena, Arkansas (a short ride over the Mississippi River from Clarksdale) in the 1930s – and by musicians who went in search of an audience. As Robert Johnson's sometime travelling companion David 'Honeyboy' Edwards told Robert Palmer, no opportunity to play and make a little money would be passed up – from setting up in the back of grocery stores on a Saturday afternoon, to improvised appearances at movie theatres between shows in the evening and late night dances in the countryside, they would go where the opportunities to play took them:

> From there, we might hop a freight, go to St Louis or Chicago. Or we might hear about where a job was payin' off – a highway crew, a railroad job, a levee camp there along the river, or some place in the country where a lot of people were workin' on a farm. You could go there and play and everybody would hand you some money. I didn't have a special place then. Anywhere was home.[4]

If the music had a single 'Great Subject', Robert Palmer observed, it was 'impermanence':

> 'The sun's gonna shine on my back door someday,' sang Tommy Johnson, hopefully. 'The wind's gonna rise and blow my blues away.' Willie Brown began his 1930 recording 'Future Blues' with these lines: 'Can't tell my future, I can't tell my past / Lord it seems like every minute gonna be my last.'[5]

The guitar, as the almost constant companion of the travelling singer, was an object of transformation; a musical instrument with an unseen power to allow the gifted and willing player to move between two worlds – the world of repression that characterized life in the South for most Blacks and the world of freedom, represented by life on the road.

The absence of social and economic mobility for African Americans in the Delta, where working on the land was the most common means of making a living, lent a certain kind of romance to the idea of travelling as a performer, and consequently to the very routes through (and out) of the Delta – country roads, highways and railroads – that would be celebrated in song, and that fulfilled a deep-seated desire for movement and freedom. For those musicians who found a way to free themselves from the need to work on the plantations, the road ultimately led to the frontiers of a new technological age that could be glimpsed in the sometimes ad hoc recording studios that were temporarily set up in big cities like Memphis (to try and sweep up the best of the burgeoning Delta blues), or in record company premises in cities like Chicago and New York. Tom Dorsey (or 'Georgia Tom', as he was known), a million-selling blues pianist in the late 1920s, recalled his time scouting down in the Delta with New York's Vocalion record company on a field trip in 1929, when the company had set up a base and a makeshift studio at the Peabody Hotel in Memphis, with the aim of reeling in as many talented blues players as they could find in the Delta:

> We'd go down in Mississippi, down in those cottonfields, we lookin' for talent. Some of the fellows who could hoot down there in the fields, they brought some of them up [to Memphis] and recorded 'em.[6]

One of the main talent scouts in the Delta was H. C. Speir, who owned a furniture store in Jackson, Mississippi, that also sold records, and who was instrumental in sending many blues singers – among them Charley Patton, Skip James and Tommy Johnson – to record with the leading record companies of the day. Speir told the man who found him in 1964, the famed blues researcher Gayle Dean Wardlow, that in those days he would

Charley Patton in disguise: 'Who sings this great new Paramount Record? Who is the Masked Marvel'? Print advert from the *Chicago Defender*, 1929.

travel all over the south looking for singers he had heard about from others that he already knew; he would nudge them in the direction of refining their songs, coaching them in the preparation of material that could fit within the limitations of 78 rpm discs.[7] It was a skill that took some work due to the fact that a 10-inch 78 rpm record could only hold about three minutes of sound per side, which ensured that once in the studio singers who had got used to improvising and adding numerous verses in live performance had to adapt quickly to the constraints of the medium, and would 'be alerted with a red warning light when time was running short':

> Sometimes novices froze when they saw the light and stopped playing immediately. In other instances, the performance finished in time, but a noticeable acceleration in tempo in the final chorus stood as a lasting testimony to the jangled nerves of the musicians.[8]

Charley Patton, for instance, recorded some of his best-known sides in Richmond, Indiana, and his last recordings in 1934 in New York, but also in Grafton, Wisconsin for Paramount Records (in 1929, as did Son House and Tommy Johnson). Robert Wilkins and Tommy Johnson were recorded in Memphis, and later Robert Johnson in San Antonio (1936) and Dallas, Texas (1937). Once acquainted with the world of recording – with its requirements for fairly long-distance travel to reach studios, and the submission to the technological demands of the recording environment – the singers of what is known as 'country blues' (a term that refers to the rural origins of Delta blues) landed firmly in the twentieth century. It is remarkable that the music that later came to be seen as characteristic of some kind of 'primal' authenticity and derived from experiences of the rootless life, was remade as a new kind of artistry through the mass-produced commodity of the phonograph record. Not only were these records designed to be played on jukeboxes and with the Victrola wind-up phonographs that had enjoyed a boom among black consumers in the 1920s, but the very styles of the blues that made it on to record were cultivated by the record companies with a wider audience in mind than the one that these singers had got used to playing for.[9] Following the success of big-selling artists like Bessie Smith, the door was opened for the male country blues recording artists of the mid- to late 1920s, 'emphatically proving that a lucrative market existed for recordings of African American blues artists'.[10] By 1927 'race records' accounted for 5 per cent of all record sales.[11]

These records are today fragments of an experience of transit between worlds that were – by contrast with genuine folk music – wholly modern; a seemingly natural outcome of the self-creation facilitated by these so-called 'rolling stones' and their 'easy riders'. The longevity of the work of singers like Robert Johnson – an inspiration for blues fanatics who would make expeditions to the South in the 1940s and '50s, and later the 1960s blues-rock explosion that originated in the UK (The Rolling Stones, Eric Clapton and others) – derives, of course, from the fact that he was also a product of a fairly well-established record industry that opened up the interchange between the Delta, a place that had, on the one hand, been seemingly untouched by modern ways and on the other, the very modern world of the record industry.

STEPPING INTO THE FUTURE

Between the 1910s and 1970 some seven million people, rural African Americans, migrated from the American South to cities in the Midwest and North; notably Kansas City, St Louis and Chicago, where the blues of the Mississippi Delta would be electrified by performers like Muddy Waters, who would bridge the two traditions – pre-war Delta (country) blues and its post-war electrified Chicago offspring. But while the Great Migration provided one of the most obvious explanations for why the Delta blues would be transformed outside of Mississippi, the music would also travel in other directions, reaching new and far-flung listeners who would further contribute to its legacy through their own adaptations of its themes and outlook.

By the 1950s, legions of amateur record collectors and blues enthusiasts swept the Delta in search of old 78s and information about the mysterious figures whose names appeared on the records they had already managed to beg, borrow or steal. Reports from their expeditions would appear in the liner notes of reissued recordings – usually compilations made directly from whatever 78s had been rescued – and in blues collectors' magazines. In the case of enthusiasts such as Bernard Klatzko and Gayle Dean Wardlow, who went in search of Charley Patton and revealed some of the earliest information about his life and the world he inhabited in the Delta of the 1920s, these reports have the air of highly charged travel journals. They recounted the adventures of indefatigable amateur detectives consumed by their own never-ending road trip, which – 40 years later – still make for fascinating reading. 'We were driving north on u.s. 49', Klatzko and Wardlow wrote of the hunt for information about Charley Patton:

We had passed Yazoo City and the Yazoo River, the southeastern gateway to the Delta region. We swept up past Louise, Midnight, and Silver City to Belzoni. It was near the cotton fields outside Belzoni where I first caught the whiff of the poisons that fill the air . . . Belzoni (locally, 'Belzona') is a neat, clean town with recently built, modern shops and well-kept homes with trim lawns. The 'Quarters' – Mississippi-ese for Negro quarters – consisted of several rows of unpainted shacks. In 'High Sherriff,' Charlie Patton sings, 'When the trial's in Belzona / Ain't no use feelin' proud' . . . There must have been clues to Patton's past in the courthouse there, but it was Sunday and everything was shut down.[12]

The search for people who knew Charley Patton, thus recounted, took place through a fevered itinerary of off-the-map tracts of farm housing, interstate highways and country byways, punctuated by tireless door-to-door inquiries – all in a place that still seemed somehow strange and foreign in its old ways. They soon brought a knowledge that would reach far beyond the blues initiates of the Delta, and brought it into a different kind of existence through a variety of commercial and artistic interchanges made possible by the routes in and out of the Delta (highways, railroads), and the interest of later waves of blues pilgrims who headed to the South looking for this seemingly timeless music and its performers.[13] Yet as much as the music seemed to give voice to a common language, regarded by W. C. Handy – seemingly the first stranger to communicate its existence to the world outside the Delta – as coarse and unrefined, the distinctive voices of the singers we know today emerged. Charley Patton, 'frail and short', who 'walked with a limp', is transformed in the contemporary imagination into an imposing presence, simply by virtue of the aura that comes off of those recordings made at the turn of the 1930s.[14] He has been described as having 'the voice of a giant' on account of the deep, bottomless growl that echoes from those ancient-sounding recordings, lending to a perception among the early blues enthusiasts of the 1950s that he was as real and authentic as Delta blues got – a 'sepulchral' presence 'from another world'.[15] And that is the power of recorded *sound* – it exists as the fragment of times, places and cultures that may have vanished, but which are able to rise to life again.

One route the record collectors and amateur detectives who would be foremost in leading the recovery and preservation of this music took in and out of the Delta was the so-called 'blues highway', U.S. 61. Running all the way from Louisiana in the south to the Canadian border at Minnesota, it is a road that has itself assumed a near-mythical status in the history of American music, and much else besides. It was on Highway 61 at Clarksdale, for instance, where Bessie Smith, the 'Queen of the Blues', died in

The crossroads at Clarksdale, Mississippi, where u.s. routes 61 and 49 meet. It has been suggested that this could be the mythical crossroads that the Robert Johnson legend is centred on.

a car wreck, and where Martin Luther King was assassinated in a roadside motel in 1968.

Through the north–south arteries of the u.s. highway system – including highways 49, 51 and 61 (all the subjects of multiple songs) – the music of the South flowed into new territories and met with new encounters. Tupelo, Mississippi, the birthplace of Elvis Presley, can be found on the North Mississippi Hill region that borders the Delta; and it was just off Highway 61 further north in Memphis that Presley lived as a teenager, worked as a truck driver, and recorded his first groundbreaking singles for

Sam Phillips's Sun label – records that borrowed from both the blues and hillbilly country music to forge a new sound that would be called rock 'n' roll.

Phillips was a pivotal figure in the development of American music, and happened to be in the right place at the right time. Memphis was something of a staging post on the way to the northern cities for those leaving behind the 'treadmill of share-cropping' for the 'robotic grind' of northern factories.[16] 'The city had something that was less common in the countryside', Robert Gordon notes – electricity:

> In the rural juke joints a lone acoustic guitarist or a band of all acoustic instruments could propel a crowd to madness, but in the city, the musicians adapted their styles . . . They plugged in.[17]

And when they did, Sam Phillips was listening, aware that he might have it within his abilities to free up these performers in ways that would allow them to hear a side of themselves they had never really acknowledged.[18] Among the Delta exiles who found themselves in Memphis in the late 1940s and early 1950s were Howlin' Wolf, B.B. King, Bobby 'Blue' Bland and Junior Parker, some of whom could be found on Beale Street, the centre of the city's musical nightlife, and later wound up in Sam Phillips's new studio, the Memphis Recording Service.[19] Before his studio was up and running, the budding producer had worked in radio, recording and playing the popular big band music of the time. But despite living in combustible times, when encouraging the mixing of black and white people could get a person killed, he knew black music and he knew it appealed to whites, and he had his eye out for the kind of opportunities that might give him his big break. Realizing the risks involved in all of this, he covered his occupational bets; in what today might seem a bizarre example of spreading his risk of failure, he took up evening classes that might provide future opportunities in an array of interesting and non-musical fields, including engineering, podiatry and embalming.[20]

In fact, while Elvis Presley would be the most famous of Phillips's protégés, he was merely one of numerous performers who passed through his studio between January 1950 and June 1954, the date claimed as the birth of rock 'n' roll proper, when Elvis Presley's first record, 'That's All Right, Mama', was recorded – an electrifying combination of hillbilly country, blues and the 'nervous rhythmic shake' that Elvis seemed to embody and which 'propelled so many of the Sun sides' Phillips produced.[21] But, landmark as that record (coupled with the equally remarkable 'Blue Moon of Kentucky') was, Phillips probably had another claim to having been present at the birth of rock 'n' roll just a few years earlier. Many, indeed, give the accolade of the 'first rock 'n' roll record' to another song recorded in his Memphis studio. That song was 'Rocket 88' – recorded in 1951 by Jackie Brenston and His Delta Cats. They hailed from Clarksdale, Mississippi, hence the 'Delta Cats' tag. But it was a manufactured name, designed to try and take another, undercover, stab at the big time; the band who recorded what is claimed by some as the first example of rock 'n' roll were, in fact, Ike Turner and His Kings of Rhythm, a rollicking R&B outfit that eschewed the deep blues of the Delta for a more uptown sound influenced by big bands and music being made in New York and California at the time. On 'Rocket 88', sideman Jackie Brenston was featured as the lead singer – a decision made by Phillips, who didn't think that Ike Turner had a strong enough presence as a lead singer.

In 1951 Ike Turner – later to achieve worldwide fame in the 1960s with the band he led featuring his wife Tina – was still a young man, just twenty years old, but he had been involved with music for some time. At the end of the 1930s, as an eight-year-old boy, he began hanging around at the studios of WROX in Clarksdale,

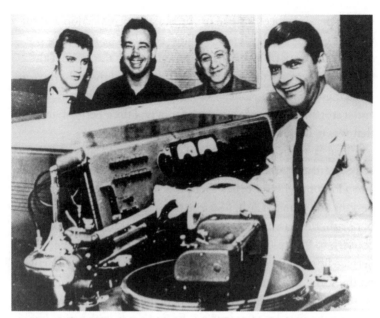

Elvis Presley, bass player Bill Black, guitarist Scotty Moore, and Sun Records and Memphis Recording studio head Sam Phillips, 1954.

which broadcast out of the Alcazar Hotel. In time, Turner would become a disc jockey there himself. Clarksdale, at the crossroads of routes 49 and 61 in the heart of the Delta, had long been a magnet for aspiring 'young black musicians who fled surrounding plantations' and moved to the town, 'where department stores, restaurants, barbershops, and WROX radio station were beacons of hope and excitement'.[22]

By the time that 'Rocket 88' was recorded, Turner had already established one of the hottest and most devastating bands around, and was also acting as both a talent scout for California's Modern Records and Chicago's Chess Records, and a producer at Sam Phillips's studio in Memphis (where he brought one of his discoveries, B.B. King). Phillips recorded a wide range of acts from around Memphis, and held fast to the idea of capturing unique performances instead of the pursuit of perfection and the niceties of making flawless sounding records. The key thing was to find that spark of ingenuity that might ignite the room if the combination of talents and influences contained the right mixture of elements. He also pioneered the use of studio effects like echo and distortion to provide a setting for 'a real time performance that was in itself somehow extraordinary'.[23]

That fact that countless musicians who would later go on to achieve greater fame elsewhere seemed to pass through his doors – in addition to Elvis Presley there was Jerry Lee Lewis, Carl Perkins and Johnny Cash, to name but a few – almost like lost opportunities passing before his own eyes, was initially of little concern to Phillips. The revolving door of his Memphis Recording Service fitted in fine with the modus operandi before Elvis arrived on the scene and hinted at greater possibilities. At the time, he was happy to make deals with independent record labels and lease to them the masters of recordings he had made with artists he found in and around Memphis.

'Rocket 88', which would be released by Chicago's Chess Records and become that label's first national number one hit, stakes its claim to being the first rock 'n' roll record because of its driving 4/4 beat and distorted guitar, which was a sound more or less unknown in 1951. That abrasive and seemingly uncontrolled sound, later to become fairly common in the 1960s when fuzz pedals and other sound effects were introduced, came about – like so many of the innovations in recorded music – entirely by accident. As Ike Turner and his band were travelling from Clarksdale to Memphis along Highway 61, his guitar player's amplifier fell off the roof of the car, where it had been sitting with the band's other luggage, puncturing one of the speaker cones. When it was later subjected to some ad hoc repair work in the studio, and stuffed with newspaper to try and cover those parts of the cone that were punctured, the speaker just happened to produce a raspy distorted tone that Sam Phillips loved. It was one of those accidents that seemed to be what made the difference between a great record and the same old stuff that had been heard a million times. 'I don't know anything about producing records,' Phillips once said, 'but if you want to make some rock 'n' roll music, I can reach down and pull it out of your asshole.'[24] His job was to conjure up the right kind of ambience and to prime the performers to capture something that, though submitted to the deadening process of endless takes, was in its essence entirely alive and of the moment.

Whether or not 'Rocket 88' was the first rock 'n' roll recording is a matter that might never be resolved, but there is no doubt that it rocks hard for the time. It also seems fitting that a band from the Delta, even though they had turned to a new urban sound, understood the power of movement as a most appropriate theme to lay over the driving sound. In lyrical, if not musical, terms – with the car as the vehicle for some hell-raising fun – it was, Robert Palmer argued, a clear descendent of Robert Johnson's 'Terraplane Blues', a song in which the car serves as a metaphor for sexual potency.[25] But 'Rocket 88' was all the more timely for the fact that it reflected the new importance that the car was to take on in the minds and lives of young people in those years: a space of seemingly infinite freedom and refuge from the domestic, parental environment of the home, and in which the radio served up the kind of music that seemed to exist as the embodiment of the desires of young people of all backgrounds to be free.

Phillips, who grew up in Florence, Alabama, with the voices of the cotton fields in his ears, knew that there was a lot of music to be found out there, and was 'familiar with the sounds the city slickers gawked at'.[26] Of the exiles who had left the Delta during the Great Migration, Chester Burnett – better known as Howlin' Wolf – was the one he held in the highest esteem. He had been brought to Phillips's Memphis Recording Service at the turn of the 1950s after being spotted by Ike Turner when he was scouting for Chess Records. At that time, Howlin' Wolf – the one-time protégé of Charley Patton – had a radio show in West Memphis and played electric blues with a large band that also featured brass players. On the rear sleeve of one of Wolf's recordings of 1951, 'Well That's Alright', which never saw a release at the time but was reissued some years later on Sun Records, Phillips testified to the power of the towering bluesman, claiming he could do nothing other than sing with 'his damn soul':

> When I first heard him, I said, 'This is for me. This is where the soul of man never dies.' He was about six foot six, with the biggest feet I've ever seen on a human being. Big Foot Chester is one name they used to call him. He would sit there with those feet planted wide apart, playing nothing but the French harp [harmonica], and I tell you, the greatest show you could see today would be Chester Burnett doing one of those sessions in my studio. God, what it would be worth to see the fervor in that man's face when he sang.[27]

Phillips had been a high school dropout, but he lacked nothing in the way of enterprise, and wanted to record what he thought was the best music around, regardless of what colour its performers were. Ultimately, however, with segregation a daily reality in Memphis and the South, many of the black artists that he recorded were lured to northern cities like Chicago, where the social and political climate was less tense, and where the idea of blacks and whites working together did not appear so revolutionary. Losing Howlin' Wolf to Chess Records – who persuaded the singer to move to Chicago – prompted Phillips to create his own label, Sun Records, whose first and biggest discovery was Elvis Presley. And when he lost Presley to RCA Records, who bought out his contract, he found others.

Perhaps the finest example of Sam Phillips at work that can still be heard today is in one of those passing moments before the creative act took over, when by chance the tape running in the background captured the remarkable and hilarious session chatter just before Jerry Lee Lewis's 'Great Balls of Fire' was recorded, in 1957. Lewis, who seemed forever caught between trying to be good and being a sinner, damned to hell – thinking his own rock 'n' roll as the work of the Devil – was having doubts about what he was setting out to do, and clearly concerned that what would be unleashed by 'Great Balls of Fire' might be the eternal flames of damnation. Phillips tried to get Lewis to see it another way:

> 'Jerry. Jerry. If you think that you can't, can't do good if you're a rock and roll exponent –'
> 'You can do good, Mr. Phillips, don't get me wrong –'
> 'Now wait, wait, listen. When I say do good –'
> 'You can have a kind heart!'
> 'I don't mean, I don't mean just –'
> 'You can help people!' Lewis is now chanting a refrain.
> 'You can save souls!' responds Phillips.
> 'No! No! No! No!'
> 'Yes!'
> *'How can the Devil save souls? What are you talking about?'*[28]

HIGHWAY 61 REVISITED

The sounds of the American south – not only the Delta blues, but the Louisiana rock 'n' roll of Little Richard and Fats Domino, and the songs of another wanderer, country star Hank Williams – were carried by the powerful broadcast signals of radio stations in Memphis and further south, and reached parts of the United States that were close to the Mississippi River, which ran alongside Highway 61 for most of the road's route south to north. It was this music – blues, folk, country and rock 'n' roll – that would be the inspiration for Bob Dylan's desire to break out of his hometown of Hibbing, Minnesota, a 'nowhere' located right at the end of Highway 61. The highway itself would be reimagined as the biblical killing ground where God metes out justice in one of Bob Dylan's groundbreaking mid-1960s records, *Highway 61 Revisited* – a metaphor, some have suggested, for Dylan's own symbolic disconnection from his family roots and folk past, and identification with the idea of transformation symbolized by the 'blues highway' that ran right through his hometown, but whose legends were hung over the parts of the road many miles further south.

As early as he had aspirations to become a musician, Bob Dylan was imagining himself into a new life, one that could be transformed by escaping the confines of humdrum Hibbing. His ambition on graduating high school – as recorded in a 1959 yearbook – was 'to join Little Richard'.[29] While still at high school he would claim to have played piano with Bobby Vee, a teen star of the day, which was partially true – he had bashed out a few songs with Vee and his band for a couple of days in Fargo, North Dakota, in 1959, after bluffing that he had just come off the road playing piano in the band of country star Conway Twitty, who had already enjoyed Number One hits on the nation's country charts.[30] It was the 1950s – who knew what Conway Twitty's piano player looked like. Dylan's bluff worked. Twitty, coincidentally, came from the other end of Highway 61 – from Friar's Point, the stomping ground of Robert Johnson in the 1930s – right in the heart of the Mississippi Delta, a few miles from Clarksdale, and had started out playing rock 'n' roll for Sam Phillips at Sun Records.

By the time Bob Dylan had reached New York's Greenwich Village in 1961 he had manufactured an entirely fictional past that was modelled upon the hobo adventures of Woody Guthrie, as told in his autobiographical book *Bound for Glory*, and undoubtedly further inspired by 'the Beat affinity for the road' – an attitude towards experience 'that braves anything as long as movement is encouraged'.[31] As such, Dylan became the pre-eminent representative of the values of a new generation, driven initially by rock 'n' roll and its embodiment of this resurrected Beat ethos and – as an artist – committed to self-exploration as the highest value in life. 'The image of the troubadour, whose ballads and broadsides exemplify the romance of being "on the road" was successfully harnessed' by the youthful Dylan.[32] If such a posture was characteristic of a great many of his generation, what made Dylan stand out – aside from the songs – was the extent to which he set about disowning his own past and in doing so created a backstory of pure myth. In a newsletter of New York's Folklore Center published in November 1961, a short biography announces Dylan's first major concert in the city at Carnegie Chapter Hall on 4 November 1961, and lays out the story of his life so far – a mixture of fact and fantasy – as it would be repeated on many occasions until he was found out in 1963:

> Bob Dylan was born in Duluth, Minnesota in 1941. He was raised in Gallup, N.M., and before he came to New York earlier this year, he lived in Iowa, South Dakota, North Dakota and Kansas. He started playing Carnivals at the age of fourteen, accompanying himself on guitar and piano. He picked up the harmonica about two years ago . . . He learned the blues from a Chicago street singer named Arvella Gray.[33]

The story was further embellished with details he would later describe in his autobiography, *Chronicles* (which itself has been subject to accusations that it is significantly fictional), as 'pure hokum – hophead talk'.[34] Not least among the sources of this disinformation were the press releases of Columbia Records, stating that Dylan had spent most of his life on the road, where

A Columbia Records advert for Bob Dylan, 1962.

he accumulated the experiences that were now tumbling out in the words of songs that could be found on his first two albums, a good many of which are – indeed – songs about being on the move and living a kind of hobo existence, as well as covers of old blues and folk songs. Indeed, John Hammond, the famous Columbia Records producer who signed Dylan, took him on after hearing his song 'Talkin' New York', a long and rambling ode to the travelling life that presumed to explain how he had managed to wind up in New York.

One of the first things John Hammond did after bringing Dylan to Columbia was to give him an advance copy of a new release that he had been instrumental in putting together – *King of the Delta Blues Singers* by Robert Johnson, a singer then all but unknown, which Columbia had released in 1961. Hammond told Dylan that he considered him to be part of that tradition of old American blues and folk, and at around the same time, Hammond had been in more direct contact with it, acting as producer on an album with the rediscovered Son House, former associate of Charley Patton and Robert Johnson's one-time guitar teacher. As Dylan wrote in *Chronicles*, the Robert Johnson record made an immediate impression on him and opened up new possibilities for artistic expression, as it would for a generation of young musicians and songwriters:

> The stabbing sounds from [Johnson's] guitar could almost break a window. When Johnson started singing, he seemed like a guy who could have sprung from the head of Zeus in full armor. I immediately differentiated between him and anyone else I had ever heard. The songs . . . were so utterly fluid.[35]

Following the example of these early blues singers, touring performers of the 1960s and '70s not only spent significant amounts of their lives 'on the road', but celebrated the life this entailed as some kind of calling or vocation. In his early career, Bob Dylan – under the sway of the train-hopping Woody Guthrie – doubtless attempted to fast-track his own legend by embellishing his own past with tales of being an itinerant folksinger and sometime circus carny who landed in New York after learning his craft from various vagabonds and drifters. He soon felt trapped, however, by the expectations of the new folk revival that he was helping to invigorate, and 'bristled at being tied to his times'.[36] Dylan, David Dalton suggests, 'is a method actor who sees his life as an emblematic movie. You make a song real by becoming the character – the voice – who's singing it.'[37] Conforming to anything went against his character, which had emerged under the influence of not only the Beats and the unregulated explosions of '50s rock 'n' roll, but – if his songs are any kind of evidence – the shadow cast over American life by a host of 'outlaws, drifters, hustlers, and poets', who might be seen as 'psychic guides through the wilderness' that was America, this 'country without a past, without a history'.[38]

It all came to a head at the Newport Folk Festival in July 1965, when Dylan appeared sporting an electric guitar and the kind of look that served as a statement of intent. Much has been written about this occasion and its significance as a cultural moment, but in terms of describing how Dylan's own journey appeared to the witnesses who observed a shocking transformation take place before their own eyes, the sparse concert notes of the New York music critic Robert Shelton, an early supporter of Dylan, seem to convey a sense of shock, and probably indicate how dumbfounded the audience must have been by the appearance of this '(reluctant) prophet of the folk boom' in this time and place.[39] Among the few scrawled notes pencilled into Shelton's pocket notebook were the scraps of what must have seemed the important points to mention:

Dylan on at 9:25
2 = Like A Rolling Stone
Leather jacket
Someone yells "Bring Back Cousin Emmy"
Dylan = Leather & black shirt[40]

'Like a Rolling Stone' was already on the radio, so the full band treatment might have come as little surprise. The sight and noise of Dylan, however, may have temporarily confused Shelton, as it seems that he was wearing an orange shirt. But the Beatnik look was a sign of things to come, matched by further evidence of the Beat influence on the album Dylan would go on to record in the following weeks, *Highway 61 Revisited*. Its rear sleeve contained a long, densely presented text – stream-of-consciousness style, perhaps influenced by works like Gregory Corso's poem

Freewheelin' and heading for the future: Bob Dylan and friend on a motorcycle, 1964.

'Bomb' (1958) – alongside a few snapshots of the singer with electric guitars in the studio.

The older generation who had nurtured the folk boom that was represented by the large crowds at Newport – Pete Seeger, Alan Lomax and others – saw all their work 'slipping away in a haze of marijuana smoke and self-indulgence' as Dylan's work increasingly journeyed further inward.[41] When this took him to his own crossroads, Dylan felt pulled in the direction of freedom and the blank prospects offered by the unknown future. *Highway 61 Revisited*, released in August 1965, was made up of nine songs that 'track the moment where he finally pieced together his divergent pasts':

> the early love of R&B and rock & roll . . . his immersion in American traditional music, folk, blues, country, Woody Guthrie, Robert Johnson, Hank Williams, and Harry Smith's *Anthology of American Folk Music*; his reading of poetry and novels, John Steinbeck, Rimbaud, Bertolt Brecht, Allen Ginsberg, and Jack Kerouac.[42]

What Dylan became was a kind of explorer of the American prospect in all its confused and dazzling possibilities, which carried him backwards and forwards – drawing on the past and this stew of influences and, in the case of 'Like a Rolling Stone' and *Highway 61 Revisited*, inventing something new: rock music, as distinct from rock 'n' roll, was a form of expression that aspired to a kind of artistic integrity and self-consciousness that transformed experience – the fast-changing modern world that one might absorb – into the material of play. 'I've stopped composing and singing anything that has either a reason or a motive to be sung', Dylan said of his move beyond the confines of so-called 'topical' songwriting, in early 1966:

> My older songs, to say the least, were about nothing. The
> newer ones are about the same nothing – only seen inside
> a bigger thing, perhaps called Nowhere.[43]

In fact, as he grew into his older years, Dylan's desire to escape
the attempts of fans and critics to box him into some version
of 'Bob Dylan' caused him to muse on the attractions of not
expressing himself at all – if it was up to him, he said, he wouldn't
write songs anymore; he'd just record songs by Charley Patton,
that other man of many voices, who wore a mask and operated
under a pseudonym.[44] And while Dylan never went that far – he
did, though, record some variations of Patton's songs 'High Water
Everywhere' and 'Pony Blues' – it became clearer that Dylan was
'up to the ears in the shared imagery' of Delta bluesmen like
Charley Patton, and only too aware of the power of the mythic
that continued to draw listeners back into that past.[45] Others of
Dylan's generation, who perhaps seem less obviously connected
to this same tradition, nonetheless inherited something of the
spirit of the blues, and took it in new directions while remaining
in thrall to a life of movement and uncertainty.

5 JIM MORRISON'S HIGHWAY TO OBLIVION

HOBO IN THE DREAM DUMP

'There was everything and everyone', Joan Didion wrote. The occasion was a recording session by The Doors in 1968 that she had somehow managed to find her way into. It was during the fraught period that surrounded the making of their third album, *Waiting for the Sun* – the so-called 'difficult' third album, as it used to be known in the music business, the point at which many rock bands seemed to run into trouble. All the early repertoire is gone, buried on those first two albums, leaving – often – the dreaded blank canvas of the third album, and the prospect of *working* in the studio (rather than going in and just slamming down the songs that you had been playing with regularity for the last year or two). There was everyone and everything apart from Jim, 'the fourth Door', the cosmic hobo. He didn't turn up again. 'The lead singer, Jim Morrison', Didion noted in a dispatch intended to inform the unknowing, was 'a 24-year-old graduate of UCLA who wore black vinyl pants and no underwear and tended to suggest some range of the possible just beyond a suicide pact'.[1] Jim was missing, but no one was surprised.

No sooner had The Doors come to national prominence than Jim Morrison, the focal point of most of the attention the band would attract in their short and eventful career, wanted to disappear, to vanish without a trace.[2] 'Light My Fire', a song from their first album, was number one on the U.S. Hot 100, but Morrison was not happy with the level of exposure that came with the sudden success that had overcome these apparently doom-laden natives of Los Angeles in early 1967. Everybody wanted a piece of Jim. Girls pawed at him, thrust their hands into his crotch if they could get close enough, or tried to grab some hair as a souvenir. The truth may have been that fame was a particular kind of experience that couldn't be anticipated, and which fell short of the hopes he had entertained when he seemed to – with the benefit of hindsight, at least – accidentally end up as the lead singer in the one band that would overwhelmingly come to represent the flip side of late 1960s optimism.

The fact was that Morrison shouldn't even have been in Los Angeles that summer of 1965 when he found himself, for the first time, assuming the unlikely position of the front man in a rock band. He was supposed to be on his way to New York after his graduation from UCLA's film school, following a plan that had earlier been mapped out. But while that road leading eastwards beckoned, the truth was that financial reality – and an unwillingness to seek help from his family – had him temporarily stuck in Los Angeles. He was broke and living on the goodwill of a friend who had an apartment in a rundown building next to the oceanfront at Venice Beach, LA's main bohemian enclave. Morrison had access to the roof of his friend's building, where he lived for the whole summer. The nights were warm, so sleeping out was easy. There was nothing up there to disturb him, alone with just his few possessions: 'a sleeping bag, an orange crate housing a few books covered with a towel to keep out the moisture', and a few other things. 'But those weren't what mattered. Next to them, lying open on the cement floor, was something more valuable than anything in the finest house in Beverly Hills – a tattered black Scholastic notebook filled with his poetry.'[3] Morrison was not eating, and his daily routine of wandering around amid the fading grandeur of Venice's abandoned canals and crumbling building facades, observing a world seemingly revolving around him as he dropped acid, ensured that he reached the kind of meditative state of being where he was able to access inspiration without the anxieties and insecurities – the writer's block – that would beset him in his final days.

But from adversity springs opportunity. These were the kind of circumstances out of which countless Americans had pulled themselves into a new existence, and Morrison – bumming like a hobo – had hung around long enough, and in the right places, to ensure that he might eventually happen upon Ray Manzarek, who until a few months' previously had just been one of his UCLA film school acquaintances. Manzarek was a couple of years Morrison's senior, and infinitely more mature.

If you can find it, and if you look closely, you can even glimpse the two future Doors together at a party that features in Manzarek's student film, *Induction* (1966). But while they had known each other, Manzarek later described their post-UCLA encounter at Venice Beach in the kind of terms that seemed to underline the transformation that Morrison had undergone that summer, living on the roof of that apartment block.

Relaxing down by the ocean at Venice Beach one morning, 'sitting in the sun, just being a bum, smoking a joint', Manzarek witnessed a vision of his future that saw beyond the directionless Morrison he had previously known; this was the image of a Greek god-like Morrison who seemed to just step off of the ocean, as if he had just found a way back – in the words of the first song he would share that day, 'Moonlight Drive' – from a nocturnal swim out to the end of the horizon to touch the dipping moon. As the vague outline of this person walked towards him, like a shadow in front of the glistening ocean, passing through the shallow, lapping waves, and kicking up the water, it seemed to Manzarek that twinkling stars were just lighting off his toes.[4]

Back then, in the long hot summer of 1965, Morrison – then only 21 years old – had already begun to write words and melodies,

The Doors (L–R: Jim Morrison, Robby Krieger, Ray Manzarek and John Densmore) at the oceanfront in Venice, California, during a photo session for their album *Morrison Hotel*, 1969.

songs for an imaginary band, he said. As it happened, Manzarek was already playing keyboards in a Surf band with his brother Rick – they were called Rick and the Ravens. In the space of a few months they would become The Doors, along with two musicians from Manzarek's Transcendental Meditation class – John Densmore, a drummer, and Robby Krieger, a guitarist – who shared the organ player's love of jazz, blues and Beat literature. Together they soon began to create something new; a 'patricidal fusion of psychedelic rock, cool jazz, Mississippi blues and classical piano'.[5]

Which is to say that The Doors sounded like no one else, and certainly like none of the bands then popular on the Los Angeles scene – the likes of The Byrds, The Mamas and the Papas, and Sonny & Cher. Even on that day at Venice Beach when Manzarek proposed that he and Morrison start a band, he recounted that the words that Morrison sang – the words to 'Moonlight Drive' – caused an immediate reaction and that 'as he was singing I could hear the chord changes and the beat; my fingers immediately started moving. I could hear weird, strange, spooky notes.'[6] The two resolved to form a rock 'n' roll band and, in keeping with the popular barometer of success, 'make a million dollars'.[7] As many have observed, the music The Doors would make seemed immediately to connect to something that had a long history in the culture of Los Angeles; a version of the kind of *noir* sensibility that projected a view of the city in opposition to how it had been characterized by successive generations of natives – the so-called 'boosters' – who, consciously or otherwise, sold Southern California as the new Eden.[8] For The Doors, it was a time (the 1960s) and place (America, Los Angeles) of darkness that was paradoxically obscured by the sunshine, which continued to feed the dreams that drew generations of exiles out westwards.

And, of course, at the centre of the migrations to Southern California from the early 1910s was Hollywood, 'one of the most intensely symbolic, emotionally valent landscapes in America . . . a state of mind, a self-actualizing myth'.[9] It provided, through the wonders of cinema, images that sustained countless dreams of self-improvement and transcendence; dreams concerned with just about anything. It was about the mere idea of even being allowed to dream; 'dreams about mobility, an improved life, romantic love, a better home, a more creative occupation, travel, leisure' and 'excitement of all sorts'.[10]

The contrast to all of this, found in the so-called *noir* visions of the place, and seen in the literature and film of California, peered beneath the surface and reported on a world that came out to play when the sun went down, where the dream often seemed to run out. Literary *noir*, for instance was found 'in books like Nathanael West's *The Day of the Locust*', which was where, Mike Davis argues, the other side of life was revealed in all of its spectacular cultural dimensions. There and elsewhere, the dream of Los Angeles that had been so alluring turned out to be the source of disillusionment:

> Hollywood became the 'Dream Dump', a hallucinatory landscape tottering on apocalypse, while in successive Chandler novels the climate ('earthquake weather' and mayhem inspiring Santa Ana winds) was increasingly eerie; there were even 'ladies in the lakes.'[11]

'Moonlight Drive', the song that inspired the formation of The Doors, was – in lyrical terms especially – a perfect example of this dark rock 'n' roll vision. Crooning like Sinatra, Morrison delivered 'a dark ode to the Pacific, which turned Los Angeles back into a city of night and encapsulated the menace which would become the group's stock-in-trade'.[12] The very sound the instrumental players in the band would make, it seemed, perfectly matched Morrison's own existential unease – a dual identity that manifested itself alternately in his very inability to feel settled, and his reckless submission to the seemingly limitless ways he could spend his time pushing against any boundaries he could find, real or imaginary.

The music of The Doors, he would say, gave rise to something akin to those anxieties. 'The feeling I get', he told one interviewer, 'is of a heavy, sort of gloomy feeling. Of someone not quite at home with themselves; someone not quite relaxed.'[13] This un-homeliness – the feeling of being in some way cut adrift and left to swirl in confusion – was a Doors speciality, reflected in the admixture of musical and lyrical elements that make up some of the best examples of the kind of atmospheres they created. There is 'The Unknown Soldier', one of the best songs from those sessions witnessed by Joan Didion in 1968, with its nightmarish fairground organ, martial drumming and shouting, which together achieve a sense of claustrophobia; or the twisted and almost malevolent rolling guitar line of 'The End'. It is there, too, in the restless feel of unwelcome leavings that perfectly soundtracks Morrison's almost cinematic or 'scenic' imagery in 'Riders on the Storm', a song that seems to draw the listener into the impossibility of truly being at home in this world. The travails and dangers that are inherent in being cast out are apparent in the feeling that the narrator of the song could – on the way out, leaving it all behind – be transformed from victim to perpetrator, into the 'killer on the road'.

The Doors, for the short five years or so that Morrison fronted them, were an opportunity for the kind of self-reinvention that may have been an inevitable consequence of an upbringing that was marked by little constancy aside from change itself – another place, new friends, different schools. But for a dreamer like Morrison, it was also the opening up of future possibilities. While The Doors may have gone down in history as one of the defining bands of '60s Californian counterculture, and one of the seminal Los Angeles bands, Morrison – like so many who had made it in the city – was an outsider; not so hard in a city that was historically made up of migrants, but made more interesting by the fact that his outsider status seemed to be a permanent mark of his identity.

MR MOJO RISIN'

He was the child of solid and respectable parents who, according to the conventions and standards of the 1950s, had brought him up to be a good and dutiful son, a nice boy with a short crew cut and good manners. The difference was that the Morrisons weren't like those stereotypical suburban middle-class families of the post-war years – rather the opposite. The entire family existence was of temporary arrangements likely to be torn up at short notice, more or less, unsettled and rootless. On top of that, Jim, like thousands of others of his generation, was also shaken out of the confines of conventional expectations by rock 'n' roll and the loosening it worked upon American society in the 1950s. It was a decade that saw 'a major welling up of confessional and personal expression', highlighted by the success of rock 'n' roll and the Beat movement.[14] At the centre of this cultural shift was a new understanding of self-potential, where 'improvisation and emotional volubility became hallmarks' of the culture; 'from song and poetry to painting and theatre'.[15]

In common with many others who felt alienated by their upbringing – Bob Dylan was another – Morrison latched onto, and was carried away by, the exotic and thrilling music that could be found by trawling the airwaves late at night for the sounds that were pumped out by stations way down south and over the border, and that would come through more clearly at that time of day. These were stations – like XERB of Rosarito Beach in Mexico, a few miles south of the San Diego border, with Wolfman Jack broadcasting at nights and into the early hours, and XERF of Ciudad Acuña, Mexico, and Del Rio, Texas – equipped with high-powered clear channel transmitters, unregulated and able to broadcast with as much power as they wanted. Since the 1930s, these 'x Stations' ('XE' being the call sign for Mexican stations) or so-called 'border blasters' had made a great impact on music in California and the southwest, and also beyond.[16] The impact of Wolfman Jack on the youth culture of the time in California is seen in George Lucas's film *American Graffiti* (1975), where the Wolfman (playing himself in the movie) provides a soundtrack – in the music he plays and in his manic on-air monologues – to the culture of hot-rod cruising.

The mere existence of this kind of broadcasting, and the constancy of the endless voices and sounds as a presence that lodges itself in the imagination, finds some reflection in The Doors' song 'The WASP (Texas Radio And The Big Beat)', in which the 'cool and slow big beat' coming over the air is the prelude to imaginary travels into the – ominous, disastrous – 'wanderin' Western dream'.[17]

The travels of Morrison's family, which in so many ways allowed him to form an attachment to music as something that was relatively stable, were undertaken out of necessity. They had to keep moving. Not through being cast out from their home, as was the case with so many exiles and immigrants who found themselves in California, but for the more practical reason that Morrison's father – a u.s. Navy officer – regularly received new postings to bases across the country as he rose to the rank of Admiral. They moved from the South to the southwest, initially; and then the west. They settled for short periods in 'Pensacola, Melbourne and Clearwater, Florida, twice in Washington DC, and Albuquerque, New Mexico, and once each in Los Altos, Claremont and Alameda, California' before landing back in the South – Virginia – where Morrison would attend high school.[18] And, like Bob Dylan before him, inspired by rock 'n' roll and the Beats, Morrison grabbed the chance that fame presented to reinvent himself, symbolically detaching himself from his family background entirely by declaring in the band's earliest press releases that his parents were dead. Kill the parents, *start again*. Naturally.

So accustomed to having no permanent home had Morrison become that even after all the success of The Doors he would live regularly in a cheap Hollywood motel, which – by 1970 – became the centre of his imploding universe. There, just a few short years since The Doors had conquered the charts, Morrison gave the impression of being a somewhat hobo spirit who had been hemmed in by fame (and notoriety), with escalating bad habits and an assortment of hangers-on that, his bandmates perceived, were draining away his creativity. Within a short walk of the Alta Cienega motel, where he kept his room, the band had their office and rehearsal room, which provided another alternative location where Morrison would live on and off. 'Often, he was at the office when we weren't', guitarist Robby Krieger remembered. 'He even lived there sometimes, because that was his whole life. We all had lives outside The Doors, but he didn't, and he kind of resented that. He felt like he was living it 24 hours a day, and we weren't.'[19] Morrison's everyday activities took place within a small and compact area around West Hollywood.[20] Nationally and internationally famous, it was here that he had found a routine, a kind of home ground, but without actually ever seeming to be settled. He also lived modestly, and he 'could often be seen walking around . . . or idling at the Garden District, dressed like marmoreal roughtrade in his full leathers, totally unprotected, vulnerable, and seemingly comfortable in his familiar neighbourhood'.[21]

But he was also trapped by the fact that he could not escape, creatively speaking, the demands of being Jim Morrison, lead singer of The Doors, with all the expectations that went along with that. This all culminated in the infamous Miami incident, where Morrison, after berating the packed auditorium – 'you're all a bunch of fucking slaves', he screamed – was arrested and put on trial for indecent exposure. By this time, Doors concerts were regularly characterized by the presence of large deployments of local police.

In the documentary film *When You're Strange* (2010), the image of Morrison the drifter opens the story – a version of the story – of The Doors and takes as its starting point the idea that he might actually have outlived his own death in 1971. The surprising power of these scenes of Morrison looking as if he is on the run from his life in Los Angeles, were actually from a film never really completed in his lifetime, whose main title was the common abbreviation for 'highway' used in the u.s. – *HWY: An American Pastoral*. Jim and some of his UCLA friends scripted and filmed the story, in which he plays the main part; it concerns a drifter who apprehends a car that he has managed to flag down in the California desert, around Joshua Tree.

Jim Morrison onstage at Miami prior to his arrest. Still from the movie *When You're Strange*.

The film, though, is only a partial version of the screenplay that Morrison had worked up, and initially titled *The Hitchhiker*. That screenplay featured a murderous loner named Billy (again, with Morrison to be cast in the part) and 'a cast of mythic American hobos and lowlifes' that Billy meets on his travels, and then again in some kind of afterlife – a 'hobo eternity' – following his execution for murder.[22] In a careful feat of editing, *When You're Strange* suggests that Morrison never died but decided to disappear in 1971 (and perhaps escape the bad influences that had overtaken his life by then) is firmly planted in the mind of the viewer watching these almost ghostly images of the late-period bearded Morrison, listening to radio reports of his own death as he motors into the desert landscape. It is a reminder that in a sense, of course, he didn't just pass away and simply vanish in the way that ordinary mortals like you and I die. No, Jim Morrison lives on in the music, and these images, as one of those mythic dead rock stars, and in the imagination of countless seekers after his vagabond spirit. *When You're Strange*, of course, works a narrative trick upon us all, one designed to draw us into this remarkable and short life

Police waiting backstage in Miami to arrest Jim Morrison. Still from *When You're Strange*.

now made even more of a spectacle by the multiplication of enigmas – that Morrison, for instance, seems in retrospect to have announced his disappearance in the song 'LA Woman', some six months before he died. Then there is the confusion surrounding the facts of his death, including the corpse that apparently no one had seen, or at least no one who hadn't been dead already for decades. And so on.

This all helps to perpetuate the myth that first gained ground in the years following the singer's death, and which emerged, particularly, from interviews given by Ray Manzarek, who would tell of his bafflement when Morrison said goodbye in early 1971, en route to Paris, and never came back. It couldn't be that simple, could it? 'I don't know how he pulled that one off', Manzarek said enigmatically, in an interview in 1973:

> You know, I don't know to this day how the man died and in fact I don't even know if he's dead. I never saw the body . . .

there are maybe two or three people who did see the body and they are not talking.[23]

They were all soon dead, as it happens – another detail to inflame the conspiracies. As drummer John Densmore recounted many years later:

> There was talk from the very beginning that Jim faked his death. He was a real wild guy and he was so smart that he could have thought up a scheme like that, but it didn't happen, and the thing that bugs me is Ray waxed on the idea for years to build myths and sell records.[24]

But if the allure of the road has anything to tell it is that the mythical and illusory, the far-fetched and implausible, are often what motivates these uneasy creative spirits who end up knowing nothing other than the desire to avoid staying in one place for long. There is, too, a sense of complementarity between Morrison's demise and the conspiracy theories that have always swirled around the events in Paris – take your pick – and the themes of his final artistic statement, the album *LA Woman* (1970).

Whatever way you look at it, Morrison is saying goodbye to the city of Los Angeles on that album, and perhaps something more – perhaps he is slaying the demons that the city carries with it. Is that crucified woman, tethered to a telegraph pole and featured in the album artwork, supposed to be representative of the city? A fallen angel in the City of Angels? There she is, nailed to one of the masts that runs the length of the roads and highways that defined this city of automobiles, perhaps symbolic of what Morrison was leaving behind as he drove on into his future.

LA Woman, taken as Morrison's goodbye to both a life and a place, is of a piece with an existence that was formed under an undeniable aura of rootlessness. It is Morrison's heightened

An advert for *LA Woman*, *Billboard* magazine, 1971.

perceptual awareness of being 'nowhere' most of the time, cast adrift no matter what he does to try and alter the fact that it feeds his aesthetic sensibility.

It was an incident that took place on the road on one of those days, as the family were travelling through the Southwest, that he thought had shaped his outlook forever after, engendering a gloom that he never really escaped. In the songs of The Doors the spectre of this incident – in which a truckload of Native Americans, some apparently dead, had been spilled across the road – looms over Morrison's writing. He later came to believe that the spirit of one of the dead entered him. It was an event that continued, throughout his career, to crop up in interviews, and in his lyrics – in 'Peace Frog' (from *Morrison Hotel*, 1970) and 'Ghost Song' (a spoken-word performance set to music on *An American Prayer*, which the remaining Doors put together in 1978).

By 1970, after releasing six albums in three years, and with Morrison still only 26 years old, much experience had been crammed into a few short, fast years for The Doors. The early hits and artistic highs of the albums *The Doors* and *Strange Days* had been followed by albums that were more difficult in the making, less spontaneous and with Morrison already torn between this role that had given him a new start, and a desire to throw it all in and just get wasted. In fact, he seems to have spent most of his time wasted, and even when he was more together – at the time of the *LA Woman* sessions, for instance – witnesses still recount tales of him drinking entire cases of beer during a day in the studio.[25] 'Ninety percent of the time, when he was drunk,' the producer Paul Rothchild said, 'he was impossible to deal with. The other ten percent, he transcended himself, and was brilliant. The ten percent is on his records. The other ninety percent is garbage.'[26] In her essay 'The White Album', Joan Didion records the stale atmosphere at one of the band's *Waiting for the Sun* recording sessions in 1968, as the other three Doors stood around tinkering with their instruments, wondering where the hell Jim was – yet again:

> Ray Manzarek was hunched over a Gibson keyboard. 'You think *Morrison*'s going to come back?' he asked to no one in particular. No one answered. 'So we can do some *vocals*?'[27]

After six albums with Paul Rothchild as producer and Ray Manzarek as bandleader, both assuming at various times the guise of the kind of authority figures that the drunken Morrison wanted to escape, *LA Woman* – the last album The Doors were contracted to make for Elektra Records, symbolically became his ticket to a new future. The Doors, in effect, would be just one more of those detours that had pulled him all over the country during his wandering life.

Morrison's love–hate relationship with Los Angeles was expressed for posterity on perhaps The Doors' finest album, *LA Woman*. It has been cited by many, then and now, as a return to both blues roots and the kind of 'garage' rock mentality that seemed to have deserted the band on its last few albums. The often-overproduced fluff of *Waiting for the Sun* and *The Soft Parade*, in particular, had led to a sense that the band, and Morrison (whose songwriting input had diminished as Robby Krieger's increased), were at least coasting on past glories, and at worst, were finished as a potent creative force.

KILLER ON THE ROAD

On the album *LA Woman*, the blues influence is evident not just in the feel and form of songs that hark after the kind of simple and earthy sounds that influenced a generation of white rock kids – 'The Cars Hiss By My Window', 'The WASP (Texas Radio and the Big Beat)' and John Lee Hooker's 'Crawling King Snake' – but more pointedly in the themes of movement and transformation, travel, the impermanence of relationships and place, and the seeming inevitability of once again waving goodbye to home, or whatever this place had stood in for during the last decade. It is these 'road' themes that lend the album its unifying feel of being a farewell letter to the city, and to the life that Morrison had lived there. For the first time in several albums, he had also written the majority of the songs and, as his friend Frank Lisciandro said much later, half of the songs have a strong 'goodbye, I'm getting out of here, things are about to change' feel about them:[28]

> There's a thematic flow to the album. There is no doubt that Morrison is saying goodbye to a city, to a culture and to the people who had embraced him and thrust him into stardom.[29]

The album begins, ends and is cut through with the attractions of movement. From the funky celebration of impermanence that is 'The Changeling' and its declaration of the desirability of a hobo existence, to the final fading sound of the rain and thunder that envelops the weary-sounding narrator of 'Riders on the Storm', we are reminded of what Morrison, like many of his generation, took from the Beats, and Kerouac's *On the Road* in particular: a wish to be free from the constricting culture of post-Second World War American society and all the values it held close to its heart (the pursuit of material wealth, the straight respectability of men in grey flannel suits and the imperative to keep up with the Joneses) and to embrace instead 'the vagabond lifestyle – wild liquor, wild women and wild nights'.[30]

The blues-laced sounds that the band were coming up with had a lot to do with recording in the looser and less formal environment of the tiny rehearsal room below their office at 8512

Santa Monica Boulevard in Hollywood. The whole enterprise was also aided by the fact that producer Paul Rothchild – who brought out the recalcitrant, rebellious adolescent in Morrison – had departed, leaving the band to their own devices. They produced a collection of songs that were a perfect vehicle for the restless Morrison to make his final statement with The Doors. It felt like – and sounds like – a return to something that connected with Morrison's inner sense of being. 'He liked to think of himself as an old bluesman', Bruce Botnick, the album's co-producer, said. 'He was a big fan of Muddy Waters and Howlin' Wolf and all those old blues guys. He loved the truth of the songs, and the rawness [of the blues], and he related to it.'[31]

'LA Woman' itself, the centrepiece of the album, is not only a song about driving, it is a driving song – one of those pieces of music that has the power to push anyone hearing it while behind the wheel of a car to accelerate. There is a kind of oblivion in that – in driving as moving ahead, or leaving your troubles and anxieties behind, even if only temporarily. But in 'LA Woman' Morrison drives straight into the seedy night-time underbelly of a city of 'motel money' and 'murder madness'. He has a look around, and just as the band shifts tempo towards the end of the song – which provides a marked 'cinematic', or scene-shifting, effect – seems to ride the freeway out of this nihilistic vision into some kind of transcendence.

One influence on the lyrical imagery of 'LA Woman' was John Rechy's *City of Night* (1963) which, in the words of Mike Davis, presented 'the image of the city [as] a fugitive midnight hustle', a gay underworld that rises as darkness falls, something that Morrison, the breaker of taboos, would easily identify with. But more than that, the pulsating rhythm and sense of momentum created by the musicians suggests that it is the centrality of the automobile to a sense of self and place that gives 'LA Woman' the feel of being an authentic slice of life.

In that respect, what the song 'LA Woman' celebrates is the sprawl of a city long derided for its lack of a unifying culture. To drive through the city is to realize that its essence is not in some kind of fixed point, where cultural activity is nailed down and made obvious; it is found, rather, in mobility. Movement and driving define life in Los Angeles, and the culture of the car and the freeway extends from the pop song – in the work of artists from The Beach Boys to Ry Cooder – to art and cinema. As Thom Andersen shows in his playful and almost kaleidoscopic film essay, *Los Angeles Plays Itself* (2003), the association between the car and male sexual potency lies at the heart of some of the most recognizable visions of the city. In *Chinatown* (1974), for instance, Jack Nicholson's character Jake Gittes loses his car. As well as the difficulties this creates for actually getting anywhere, it is enough to serve as a sort of symbolic emasculation, so necessary to male identity is the automobile in Los Angeles.

Elsewhere, many of the city's visual artists also made cars and car culture a central focus of their work – people like Ed Kienholz (who would not only slice and dice cars into unusual sculptures, but was buried in his car) and Ed Ruscha (who painted gas stations and photographed parking lots). These 'car culture phenomenologists', as Mike Davis refers to them, understood that there was no life in Los Angeles without the cars, the roads and the freeways to pull it all together.

Maybe 'LA Woman', in its ultimately euphoric ending, chimes with what the English critic Reyner Banham identified in his description of the city as a kind of 'Autopia', a vehicular paradise that encompasses everything, all life. 'The freeway system in its totality', he wrote, 'is now a single comprehensible place, a coherent state of mind, a complete way of life.'[32] It was something reflected in Joan Didion's *Play It as It Lays*, where the character Maria finds some kind of escape from her anxieties in the amped-up madness of the freeways:

The Hollywood Freeway at dusk, 1969.

Once she was on the freeway and had maneuvered her way
to a fast lane she turned on the radio at high volume and she
drove. She drove the San Diego to the Harbor, the Harbor up
to the Hollywood, the Hollywood to the Golden State, the
Santa Monica to the Santa Ana, the Pasadena, the Ventura.
She drove it as a riverman runs a river, everyday more attuned

to its currents, its deceptions, and just as the riverman feels the pull of the rapids in the lull between sleeping and waking, so Maria lay at night in the still of Beverly Hills and saw the great signs soar overhead at seventy miles an hour, *Normandie ¼, Vermont ¾, Harbor Fwy 1*. Again and again she returned to an intricate stretch just south of the interchange where successful passage from the Hollywood onto the Harbor required a diagonal move across four lanes of traffic. On the afternoon she finally did it without once breaking or once losing the beat on the radio she was exhilarated, and that night slept dreamlessly.[33]

What would make the time-shifting perspectives of the Jim Morrison myth of *When You're Strange* more poetically apposite would be if he had, as the listener is entitled to instinctively feel at hearing 'LA Woman's' definite air of leaving town, actually left town at the end of the song, heading out on the Hollywood Freeway along Interstate 10 and into the desert to reinvent himself once again.

But those visions of Jim in the wilderness that the film has thrown up pre-date the metaphorical crucifixion of the woman who illustrates the inner sleeve of the album. Instead, they place us in the California Desert in the summer of 1969 – if we want to be factual about it. But on the other hand, it seems a truism that what is most durable in rock music always comes with its own mythic counterpart; it is about more than just the music (as the case of Robert Johnson or Bob Dylan amply demonstrates). The music is no mere empirical stuff ready to be swallowed whole – it is warped and transformed by the tales that surround it, and by the imaginary worlds that it opens a way into. So, we might wonder, why the desert figured so prominently in Morrison's imagination. Perhaps it was because it had been the home of mystics and spiritual wanderers since time immemorial.

In Morrison's film *HWY: An American Pastoral* we see an empty road in the middle of nowhere. The heat rises from the surface and 'melts' the road beyond into the air, and there is Jim Morrison, in full leathers, walking by the roadside. The Lizard King, hitchhiking his way out of Los Angeles and all the trouble that had accumulated there over the last four years. The desert is a place of exile and reversed expectations – devoid of human comforts, full of a kind of menace that is a threat to human life, a liminal zone where time and the future run out, only to be swallowed up, so to speak, by the geological time of the eternal. The hitchhiker who emerges

Jim Morrison as the hitchhiker (top) and 'killer on the road' (bottom) in *HWY*, 1969. Stills from the documentary *When You're Strange*.

from the desert has already stripped away all social norms and conventions. There is no society in the wilderness, and HWY – which provides the lyrical imagery for the highway maniac of 'Riders on the Storm', the 'killer on the road' – plays on the idea that death haunts the desert. In an echo of his childhood encounter with the truckload of Indians splayed across the road, Morrison can be seen here stopping at the scene of another accident: this time a dog lies dying in the middle of the road.

But there seem to be something more than an echo of the past in HWY – there is a prescience in the story of the killer who comes out of nowhere at that particular time and in that particular place. The desert wilderness is associated with darkness – there is nothing darker than night in a desert – and invisibility. The sight of the bearded Morrison, the dark antithesis of the hippy dream (as The Doors had so often been described) seems to anticipate the nightmare of Charles Manson who, just a few months after these scenes were filmed, set himself loose on Los Angeles from further north in the California Desert.

It was at a remote box canyon known as Barker Ranch – an apparently suitable opening into which anyone on the run might disappear – that Manson and his notorious 'Family' had temporarily vanished, escaping the reach of the Los Angeles Police Department, who were then on the trail of the perpetrators of the so-called Tate-LaBianca murders of 1969, when the Manson family attacked in the heart of Hollywood. Like an evil counterpart of the desert mystics of religious lore – who went into the desert in search of some kind of revelation from above – Manson believed himself to be within reach of 'a hole that he claimed would lead to an underground paradise'.[34] In choosing the desert as the most fitting base from which to launch a series of destructive forays into Los Angeles, Manson – consciously or otherwise – made a symbolic choice that followed in a tradition of outsiders and outlaws; people drawn to a life 'apart from all semblance of order', which was here found in the 'empty, arid and inhospitable' regions of the California desert.[35]

But unlike Manson and his Family, what Morrison wanted to destroy was not the citizens of Los Angeles, but rather himself. Towards the end of his time in LA he recorded a number of spoken word sessions, and something like death – in his allusions to the dead of night and 'A dim nothingness' – seemed to be looming more perilously than ever.[36]

HWY's imaginary hitchhiker, recast (or re-imagined) as the fleeing Morrison in *When You're Strange,* presents the visual trace of his mind for much of the time during the last years of his life. Ultimately, as we know, he would disappear to Paris, into the unknown, following Pam Courson, his long-time girlfriend who was by then in the grip of heroin. Less than a year earlier he had followed her – not entirely willingly – to London, where Pam's connection was a Rolling Stones associate known as Count Jean de Breteuil, who was then looking after Keith Richards's house in Cheyne Walk. There 'the smack flowed while Keith was away in Nellcôte, south of France, starting the sessions for *Exile on Main St.*'[37] By the time Morrison ended up in France, he too had found heroin.

But to anyone on the outside who might have picked up on the *LA Woman* vibe, and who looked close enough at what scant evidence was available as the real disappearance approached – the cover of *LA Woman,* for instance – it was noticeable that Morrison was already easing himself out of the picture. There, the over six-foot-tall Morrison seems to be sinking or diminishing in height, as his bandmates remain upright. He had had too much to drink, they say, and had to sit on a stool. But that's just the facts of that moment – the reality is that all he wanted to do was make himself appear less prominent, less of a presence, if not to completely disappear from view as soon as he could. It is clear that Morrison, as a student of romantic poetry, knew that what would last would be the records – the songs and perhaps his words, which in performance, in singing or reciting, would outlive any of the material forms they had taken, and which had associated them with this entity, Jim Morrison, the 'Lizard King'. 'Nothing can survive a holocaust but poetry and songs', he wrote towards the end of his life. 'No one can remember an entire novel. No one can describe a film, a piece of sculpture, a painting, but so long as there are human beings, songs and poetry continue.'[38]

6 ROLLING STONES, THROUGH THE LOOKING-GLASS

> The camera phalanx in the tunnels. People sitting around,
> two people asleep in a lump or tripped out or they could
> be unnoticeably dead, the endless noisy boredom of the
> tour – tunnels and runways.
>
> Don DeLillo, Underworld (1997)

ENTOURAGE

When Robert Johnson sang of the pull of the underworld at his fateful (and mythical) encounter with the Devil at some remote Mississippi Delta roadside – damned, and with his fate apparently sealed – little could he have imagined that a bunch of white boys from England would be the ones to carry on his legacy, bringing the themes of his music to a mainstream white audience. The Rolling Stones, in fact, would become so enamoured of the 'on the road' experiences of two generations of American blues singers who had seemed destined never to stay in one place – and who sang mostly about the highs and lows of such a life – that they would turn the life that their songs conjured into their own kind of culture.

The Rolling Stones would establish the benchmark for rock music as performance thereafter (on and offstage) for a period that reached from 1969 to the early 1980s. By that end point, so much had changed in rock music that it could arguably be said to mark the beginning of the end of this era of road music; this music of exile, itinerancy and roving vagabonds. This culture emerged partly as a result of its origin in a foreign land (which lent the Stones and other British bands a strange and powerful air of the exotic to many fans), and partly due to its mobility and its tendency to be transmogrified by the very places it visited and people it came into contact with. It would always be marked off from the temporal rhythms and mores, if not the laws, of conventional society. It was a miniature society on the road.

The Rolling Stones were already perceived, in terms of their influence on the youth of the day, as a more dangerous counterpart to The Beatles, and were Englishmen who had lived and breathed American music – from blues and R&B to the pop charts – since adolescence. Mick Jagger and Keith Richards, former primary school classmates later separated, discovered each other again many years later as teenagers, at Dartford railway station in Kent, both carrying records that the other recognized, by Muddy Waters and Chuck Berry. As The Rolling Stones they would bring 'the road' to life as a great carnival; a 'mad binge around America', as Mick Jagger would later describe their triennial adventures, which reached a pitch of intensity and scale of entourage that was unmatched by any other contemporaries, but which nonetheless served as an inspiration for a generation who followed them and for whom life on the road would be the embodiment of the ethos of sex, drugs and rock 'n' roll.[1] *If it was okay for the Stones*, the reasoning went, *then it is okay for anyone* (likewise the longer the Stones go on, the easier it becomes for those who are younger to continue rocking into their old age). It had to be America that would effect this transformation on The Rolling Stones, which revealed in its turn the essence and source of their music: only America would allow these latter-day colonists to roam the land from coast to coast until they could 'shake another bit' of it loose from the strictures of the kind of normality that for many was still a deadening reality.[2] As Jagger would say to the audiences on their U.S. tour of 1969, 'you have to be loose, babies.' It's what they, the Stones, were – unmoored, free – they were *rolling* stones, after all, named after the Muddy Waters song 'Rollin' Stone' (1950), and on the loose in the vast United States; a place like no other in affording them an opportunity to realize their idea of what The Rolling Stones represented.

Until The Rolling Stones had reconfigured the idea of the rock 'n' roll band on tour – which had now expanded to include a retinue of high, low and non-society types – no one had plunged quite so deeply into life on the road as a parallel existence so elaborately staged that it could constitute a new kind of culture. This culture revolved around engineering the practicalities of a mobile and itinerant life to enable a bunch of musicians to reach their peak at just around the time they had to perform onstage – a couple of hours in the day – and then live out the life that they had designed around it. As Truman Capote, one of the writers accompanying the tour in 1972, found out when trying to resist Keith Richards banging on his hotel room in the early hours of the morning ('Aw, c'mon man, come out and see what a rock 'n' roll band is really like'), the show onstage was only a prelude to what followed as the band let off steam afterwards. By the turn of the 1970s, 'the road' was envisioned as a route into a kind of nowhere that only really came to life when the carnival found its audience and went into full swing, and, like some rock 'n' roll Brigadoon: here today, gone tomorrow. And with each u.s. tour there would be something new to make the downtime on the road more bearable.

Travelling on commercial airlines was a necessity in the u.s., but also a precarious business for a bunch of funky looking vagabonds – as the sentiment of Keith Richards's song 'Connection' (1966) shows, with its allusion to the difficulties drug users faced crossing borders – so the logical step was to acquire some more private means of transportation without going back to touring by bus: a private plane. 'For the first time we travelled in our own hired plane', Richards said of the 1972 u.s. tour. It was adorned with their new emblem, the fat red lips and lapping tongue that graced the label of the band's new Rolling Stones Records label, and later the T-shirts of millions of fans for decades thereafter. 'We became a pirate nation, moving on a huge scale under our own flag with lawyers, clowns, attendants.'[3] The various members

Keith Richards, seated, on guitar, leads the backstage entourage in song (top); Charlie Watts alights from the *Lapping Tongue*, the plane that moved the Stones around the U.S. in 1972 (bottom). Stills from the film *Crossfire Hurricane* (reused footage from Robert Frank's *Cocksucker Blues*).

of this entourage who were not in the band were more than encouraged to enjoy their time, too. Terry Southern was sent to report on the tour for the influential literary weekly *Saturday Review*, where his account of the non-musical side of things became the story. 'Some of our finest moments were aboard this plane, [Tequila] Sunrise in hand, hopping from one gig to the next – Fort Worth to Houston, Houston to Nashville, Nashville to New Orleans . . . the stewardesses . . . would begin mixing the Tequila Sunrises as soon as we started up the ramp.'[4]

What the Stones managed to achieve, particularly on this 1972 tour of North America, was to set the conditions under which an almost instant mythology could be guaranteed, due to the fact that the band – Jagger in particular – recognized the importance of chronicling their existence at those moments on tour, just when it seemed to be accelerating beyond control, but all the while remaining in perfect agreement with the ideals and themes of their songs. The tour was conducted in a 'frantic atmosphere', according to an out-of-place Truman Capote, himself no stranger to the grotesque side of life. The renowned writer was one of many who were either invited onto the tour, or found themselves attached to it – socialites, drug dealers, acclaimed authors and film-makers, photographers, groupies and, of course, the more common or garden type of journalist or radio reporter, sometimes unwittingly sent into this maelstrom or spirited away on the band's private plane. Before this, no rock band, and perhaps no performer in any field of popular entertainment, had so willingly pulled back the curtain to reveal what went on backstage. Never before had those periods in transit between the innocuous and professional-sounding 'engagements' that made up the itinerary of the professional musician – cooped up in hotels, stranded at airports, driving through some remote backwoods – been so much a centrepiece of how rock 'n' roll had developed and was represented to the world outside, and as such, how it was understood as a phenomenon that exploded into the consciousness of fans, if not wider society, in a way that the music itself was incapable of doing.

Even the indestructible Keith Richards, usually at the centre of the roving circus that surrounded the band, could find it all a bit too much to bear at times. One night during the tour, as he recalled in his memoir *Life* (2010), he found himself trapped in a room full of uninvited 'bimbos' and had to resort to drastic measures to find some space in which to rest:

I kept telling them to go and they wouldn't. I wanted to clear the room and no one would listen to me. Get the fuck out. For five minutes I tried. So, *boom*. I fired a shot through the floor . . . and that cleared the room in a cloud of dust and skirts and bras.[5]

If the film of that tour, *Ladies and Gentlemen: The Rolling Stones* (1974), captures the scintillating stage act that the Stones had become, its peek-a-boo offstage counterpart, Robert Frank's never released but often bootlegged *Cocksucker Blues* (1972), presents life on the road as a marathon of tedium and banality, and of sex and drugs as the only easy (and temporary) releases from the kind of entrapment that a tour quickly becomes. The presence of Frank with his 16 mm Eclair camera, and other travelling and occasional guests, enlivened what might otherwise have been a terminally boring logistical procession across the country. A large part of being on the road, the Stones were well aware, consisted of being stuck in places where you don't really want to be, surrounded by people you might not want to have much to do with and, as Bill Wyman would complain, without home comforts, like Tetley's tea and HP Sauce – the little things. And so the circus that developed around the band's American tours was their way of trying to cope with the sheer boredom of spending large chunks of life essentially nowhere, exiles from that other kind of boredom called normality. Asked in 1989 how he would describe the first 25 years of The Rolling Stones, the eternally glum-looking Charlie Watts – filmed hanging around at an airport, no less – sighed, 'well, it's really been a lot of waiting and hanging around. Twenty years of hanging around at airports . . . and five years playing.'[6]

Robert Frank's film perfectly mirrors that understanding of he proportion of time spent, essentially, in transit in one way or the other (the time spent onstage versus all the rest), as his scenes from life on the road form the bulk of what we see in *Cocksucker Blues*, which are intercut with the briefest glimpses of the band onstage doing what it is they were supposed to do – playing to an audience. But the photographer knew that he had to blend in with this rollercoaster and become one of them, in order to make this film.

In fact, Frank would leave loaded 16 mm cameras lying around for anyone to pick up and start filming with, but even then – as the accounts of other chroniclers make clear – it was a kaleidoscope of perspectives that would provide a greater sense of the true dimensions of the tour. The more the merrier, as they say. Robert Greenfield reported in his book about the tour, *Stones Touring Party*, a typical scenario of the daily life offstage: on approaching the Canadian border on one occasion, he spied 'a hapless customs man in a log cabin with a Canadian flag' as he 'struggle[d] with manifests, crew lists and baggage numbers', and the gathering zoo that had suddenly appeared at his post.

> He has never seen people who look and act like this. Polite, co-operative, smiling but defiant, as though to say we are

A scene from Robert Frank's Rolling Stones tour movie, *Cocksucker Blues*. The film was never released, but snatches of it – as seen here – appeared in a later documentary titled *Crossfire Hurricane*.

playing your little game here but it does not apply to us.
People spill out of cars and Robert Frank has the Eclair
screwed in his face and rolling as Bill Wyman tracks him
with a Super 8. A pushy TV camera crew materializes and
tries to shove microphones in people's faces.

'Where are you from?' someone asks one of the boys with
a soundpack and a shoulder harness.

'Channel 8,' he says proudly, 'Vancouver. Where are you
from?'

'Estonia,' Keith says loftily, stalking away . . . [7]

The older Frank's assimilation within this expanded band of
troubadours and itinerants seemed complete to Greenfield –
here he was, on another occasion,

a small, compact man standing in the aisle of the bus with an
Eclair 16 obscuring his face and a just-passed joint in his hand.
In one smooth motion, the man takes the joint, hits on it, puts
it in front of the camera lens, films it, then passes it on.[8]

With hindsight, and despite the disagreements that have
ensured that this most notorious of films has never had a
commercial release, it seems blindingly obvious why the Stones
would choose Robert Frank to film life on their 1972 tour, given
that his landmark photographic work, *The Americans*, could
almost be seen as an attempt – through a different medium –
to do what the Stones would do on their great American album
Exile on Main St. (whose cover was festooned with tiny frames
shot by Robert Frank). What they did on this album was to take a
look at America in the kind of way that only interested outsiders
seemed capable of doing. Like Robert Frank, their fellow exile,
the Stones reflected America back on itself, not only revealing
layers of musical heritage, but time-travelling into a past that was

deeply rooted in the South. As a piece of recorded music, *Exile* arguably attains the kind of quality that is characteristic of a road movie – it is, if nothing else, a journey through America; and this is something that could equally be said of Frank's photography. As Jack Kerouac observed in his introduction to *The Americans*, what is taking place – what is frozen in these images – is life in all its elusive and transient banality and weirdness:

> The crazy feeling in America when the sun is hot on the streets and the music comes out of the jukebox or from a nearby funeral, that's what Robert Frank has captured in tremendous photographs taken as he traveled on the road around practically forty-eight states . . . and with the mystery, genius, sadness and strange secrecy of a shadow, photographed scenes that had never before been seen on film.[9]

Exile on Main Street is the culmination of The Rolling Stones' artistic rebirth that began with *Beggars Banquet* in 1968 – itself a compelling slice of Americana – and it is the embodiment of the values of the road, and the conjoining of influences that the idea and actuality of travel and movement can't help but engender. Along with its blues and R&B influences, the album has a significant country flavour to it. During the period of its making, Richards would often be found sitting around with Jagger and Gram Parsons – the man said to have invented country-rock in the late 1960s – 'plonking away on Hank Williams songs' while waiting for the rest of the band to arrive at Keith Richards's rented villa, Nellcôte, in the south of France.[10] The fact that the album was made on the run, so to speak (from the UK taxman), is crucial in understanding the enduring vitality of the music. Indeed, what arguably makes the music on *Exile* so timeless is its road music melange: the songs on the album not only capture an atmosphere suitable for providing the air that exiles might breathe (and no less the climate for something that they would title 'Exile'), but the music and songs are the perfect expression of those conditions, and allow for the rising sense of America that seeps through the admixture of musical elements and song styles.

At Nellcôte, Keith recalled, the band would often record right through the night. Occasionally, if the mood took hold of them, Keith, Mick, Bobby Keyes and whoever else was around in the morning, would take his little boat along the coast to a nearby town on the border between France and Italy, Menton, exercising their sense of unboundedness as they travelled, without passports or any of that paraphernalia of land-locked citizens, 'right past Monte Carlo'. On those journeys they would revel in the new space they had made for themselves,

> play something we've done, play that second mix. Just pull up at the wharf and have a nice Italian breakfast. We liked the way the Italians cooked their eggs, and the bread. And with the fact that you had actually crossed a border and nobody knew shit . . . there was an extra sense of freedom.[11]

Cooped up in the south of France, and forced to stay clear of the UK for a year, the situation was very trying for those in the band who did not entirely share Keith's wonder at the freedom of it all. Tensions mounted because the band were more or less trapped together – it was almost like being on a tour that never goes anywhere, yet seems like it will never end. The wife of guitarist Mick Taylor, Rose, later said that they really were in exile, in every way:

> If we had been at home, we could have had other people and the reality check of being with friends and family and all of that. It was very rarefied there. Tremendously isolating.[12]

MIRROR, MIRROR ON THE WALL, WHO'S THE GREATEST . . .

The real beginning of the Stones' legend as 'the greatest rock and roll band in the world' begins further back than the period around *Exile on Main St.*, in 1969. With noted art-house film-makers Albert and David Maysles in tow, the band had not only set out on a tour, but had embarked upon something that might provide a new kind of document of one of these strange, drawn-out events – the rock tours – that had revolutionized the way musicians perceived themselves, but otherwise simply came and went as the passing of the days.

On previous visits to the u.s. the band had played and moved around under very different circumstances, more in keeping with the relatively underdeveloped touring infrastructure of the early 1960s, which was still tied to the idea that live performances had to in some way be akin to the radio listener's experience. What mattered were your hits – however many you had, that's what you played. 'Sometimes we'd do two or three shows a day', Keith recalled:

> They wouldn't be long shows; you'd be doing twenty minutes, half an hour three times a day, waiting for the rotation because these were mostly revue shows, black acts, amateurs, local white hits, whatever.[13]

To contrast what the Stones' 1969 tour produced – in terms of what the attendant writers and film-makers came back with – with what went before, it appears that the band had the intention of capturing something of the day-to-day life of the modern touring rock musician, as much as they had an idea of preserving entertainment for the masses on film, or in crafting hagiographic accounts of their magnificence. The Stones did not seem motivated to have their *performances* documented much at all –

Scene from the Maysles brothers' tour movie *Gimme Shelter*: Mick Jagger (off-screen) reviews a rough cut.

although this was inevitable, thanks to the entourage they had brought with them. It was, rather, to find the means to capture the essence of the road experience. 'They weren't interested in photographs of themselves onstage', the tour photographer Ethan Russell explained later, but something less obvious, something akin to what *they*, the band, would see on the road, as opposed to what the audience would observe of the band onstage performing. The Stones 'see us' – the people outside their circle, the audience – Russell observed, and:

> the crowds at the lip of the stage, the anonymous airports, and strange encounters with people who often stare back at them as if they were cattle (in 1969 anyway, the Stones and their entourage were a freaky phenomenon).[14]

What they wanted from documents such as those produced by Russell was to see themselves *in* America, as a part of this magical landscape, this beguiling culture that they had been obsessing over since their teenage years. They weren't alone in this. As the former *Rolling Stone* reporter Cameron Crowe revealed in the wake of his fictionalized movie account of his early 1970s on-the-road experiences, *Almost Famous,* the bands he wrote about would often say to him 'write about what you see . . . they wanted to see their life mirrored back to them'.[15] Growing up in Sidcup, Kent, Keith Richards couldn't get enough of America, and wanted to be able to see himself in it. As a teenager he would 'raid the public library for books about America'. His fascination was with something more than just the music – it was about the place, and the atmosphere or milieu that those people, like Muddy Waters and Robert Johnson, had breathed in: 'the incredible explosion of music, of music as style, of love of Americana . . . there were people who liked folk music, modern jazz, trad jazz, people who liked bluesy stuff, so you're hearing prototype soul'.[16]

Gimme Shelter – the Maysles' movie – is a strange document that is as much about America seen through the eyes of the Stones and constructed around arrivals, departures and the time in-between performance, as it is about The Rolling Stones onstage.[17] And if the Maysles brothers just so happened not to be on hand to document this freaky phenomenon, it was no problem. As would be the case on the 1972 tour and on later trips around the United States as well, the band had made sure to invite along plenty of others who were only too willing to be both part of the sprawling entourage and to meticulously take note of all the little secrets that were now to be released from their confinement back there, out of sight behind the scenes. In fact, a variety of writers, reporters and photographers were on hand to show that on the road, in a rock 'n' roll band, one encountered a new kind of space where normal rules were no longer applicable. Today, it is difficult to imagine how open this world was. In our own time, the kind of touring that The Rolling Stones set in motion can perhaps still be seen as quite commonplace, but everything circumstantial that identified the culture as unique is practically gone. Modern journalists and writers really no longer have the kind of access that produced these iconic documents – the documents that underpin the myth of life on the road – simply because today everything from the daily movements of the performers to the planning of schedules and the regulation of the venues they play, is now so tightly managed and controlled. No one is giving anything away anymore, despite the appearance to the contrary that social media ubiquity offers.

The Stones seemed to give unfettered access, but this contributes, paradoxically, to the enlarged myth. Perhaps this is the result of the multiplicity of voices, viewpoints and witness testimonies. But until the 1980s, at least, this roving life that the Stones pioneered was the template for any touring band that aspired not so much to *make it*, but to be *remembered*. It was necessary to attempt to forge a myth (as U2 so self-consciously did in the film that charted their embrace of America, *Rattle and Hum*, and their plunge into the same music that inspired the Stones). Any band that aspired to have real cultural heft needed its own writers, photographers and film-makers. It was they who would embellish the story and stoke the myths. It was a kind of patronage now well out of reach of contemporary rock bands, who are lost in the noise of the too-muchness of networked and mediated modern life.

But back in 1969, as the bohemian entourage arrived in rural Alabama to record some songs, the glee taken in doing what they wanted, regardless of local expectations and sensitivities, was obvious. The supposedly incognito Stones – who at this point were breaking the law by recording in an American studio without the proper permits (they had touring permits) – did everything but remain hidden as they made their arrival, as 'writer-in-residence' Stanley Booth recounted in his seminal book *The True Adventures of The Rolling Stones*:

> At the Muscle Shoals airport there was a small terminal building with a large window through which, it seemed, most of the local population and the people from the surrounding cities of Florence, Sheffield, and Tuscumbia were looking out at the landing field. Keith [Richards] was slouching against a post in front of the window, wearing an antique Hungarian gypsy jacket, and just to start things off right in Alabama, Mick walked up in full view of the watching rednecks and kissed Keith on the cheek. 'How are you babe?'[18]

The decade was drawing to a close, but the Stones had already turned the page on the '60s. Here in Alabama at the end of their first tour for more than three years – a tour that signalled the rebirth of the band and the introduction of Mick Taylor as the replacement for Brian Jones – they would spend three days recording at the then new Muscle Shoals studio in Alabama, which was located yards away from Rick Hall's Fame Studios, where Aretha Franklin and many others had recorded some of the most indelible R&B sounds of the '60s.

In the Maysles' film, what seems to be the aftermath of the session is actually the band arriving in San Francisco for the Altamont Speedway Free Festival. As Jagger, assorted band and crew members, girlfriends and Stanley Booth are shown gathering in the room, Richards cues up a tape recording of a new song that they have just worked up during the session – 'Brown Sugar', a song that would not be released for another year and a half. The Keith Richards we see drawing on a cigarette, nonchalantly sporting a look that would serve as a textbook definition of 'rock 'n' roll' for generations of imitators, has undergone a startling

physical transformation since he was last on tour in this part
of the world. Dressed in crushed-velvet trousers, a tight-fitting
long-sleeved T-shirt and sporting a hairstyle – a kind of bird's
nest recently abandoned – that required no attention from combs .
or brushes, he is hunched over a dressing table playing with a tape
machine and, well, *digging it*.

Even Little Richard, the outrageous and self-styled 'Quasar
of Rock', was struck by the appearance of the guitarist, and
remarked, while watching the Stones film an Ed Sullivan Show
performance, that 'Keith Richards is one funky looking cat.'[19]
That was a compliment. As the first choppy chords of 'Brown
Sugar' break the chatter, he shakes his hips. Behind him Bill
Wyman – looking no less bored than he does onstage during a
performance, missing his HP Sauce and Tetleys tea, no doubt –
flicks through a newspaper. Standing in front of him, Mick
Jagger sticks out his elbows, as if to flap them like the wings of
some bird that can't fly – a chicken – about to break into one
of those onstage struts he stole from Tina Turner, much to the
amusement of Stanley Booth. It is just a few days before the
band will play one last late addition to the tour, a free concert at
Altamont Speedway some 40 miles from San Francisco – an event
that has been trailed as the West Coast Woodstock; but as we now
know, 'peace' and 'love' are not the words recorded by posterity to
describe this event.

The ability to simply announce a free concert and believe
that it would happen reflects something of the Stones' status,
if not the eagerness with which America had re-embraced them
after what was, in rock 'n' roll terms, a long absence. Since their
last visit to the U.S. in 1966 much had changed in the nature of
touring, but a lot remained the same, specifically the view from
whatever vehicle was pulling the band through its itinerary. As
Keith Richards remembered, the road seemed endless, especially
in the South:

Towns and states just went by. It's called white-line fever. If you're awake you stare out at the white lines down the middle of the road, and every now and again somebody says 'I need a crap' or 'I'm hungry'. Then you walked into these brief bits of theatre behind the road.[20]

What was new was the Stones themselves, and the sense they gave of that, in just a few years, making music had become something serious and synonymous with life itself – the idea that to be a musician meant making or playing music, and particularly being out there on the road. It was itself a way of life. 'It doesn't matter if you're 68 and bald,' Keith told Stanley Booth, 'if you can do it, there's somebody who can dig it. But if you are a rock 'n' roller, you've got to be on the stage. A rock 'n' roller doesn't exist unless he is on stage.'[21] Here, now, the Stones appeared to be the band that they had always really been, but were only now fully embracing through the shedding of the recently acquired layers of Englishness that strangely seemed to obscure their real identity in the mid- to late 1960s. There had always been evidence of 'lighter' pop songs, with a tamer Jagger singing in an English accent, featured on early albums alongside R&B cover tunes. These seem to indicate a band fumbling for an identity, concealing their blues and R&B roots while perhaps influenced by the fact that England – London, in particular – had by then become the centre of the rock and pop music world.

On *Beggars Banquet,* the band's seventh album, they seemed to step outside the shadow of The Beatles and The Kinks, who were both more essentially English, and in the process shed the pop overtones of albums like 1966's *Aftermath* (and songs like 'Mother's Little Helper', 'Lady Jane' and 'Stupid Girl'), 1967's *Between the Buttons* ('Yesterday's Papers', 'She Smiled Sweetly') and 1968's *Their Satanic Majesties Request* ('In Another Land', 'She's a Rainbow'), in favour of a kind of hard rock that was really a bluesy, countrified R&B. By the time of *Beggars Banquet*, The Rolling Stones had been reborn – as more hard-edged, with none of the quaint English flourishes (harpsichords, bells, flutes) that marked their first few albums as principal songwriters. Instead, what emerged was a more definite American identity rooted in a melange of blues, rock 'n' roll, rhythm and blues, and country that they had begun to take into new configurations, advancing on the influences. Before long they would be making the best American rock music that could be heard at the time. It was the spirit of those songs – songs like their cover of Robert Wilkins's 'Prodigal Son'– that connected the band with their blues predecessors.

In trying to raise themselves – consciously or otherwise – to another plateau, and above the Beatles-wannabe failure of *Their Satanic Majesties Request*, Jagger and Richards wrote *blues* songs, and songs that chimed with the themes and concerns of the Delta blues of 30 and 40 years earlier. Much of this transformation was put down to the fact that Richards had to learn to play slide guitar, because by 1968 Brian Jones was too far gone, his talent and expertise as a slide player and musical contributor now rapidly evaporating.

DISPATCHES FROM THE ROAD

Out on tour in the U.S., the presence of the writer Stanley Booth – roughly the same age as most of the band members, and respected as an equal in artistic terms (by Richards, if not the more circumspect-about-everything Jagger) – was indicative of the changing culture of touring and the self-conscious attempt to document and preserve events as a record of a unique period in time. Booth had earned respect for his profiles of blues singers, like Furry Lewis, and seminal figures in the development of rock 'n' roll, such as Sam Phillips. And because the tour was also being

documented by others – aforementioned film-makers Albert
and David Maysles, the photographer Ethan Russell and another
writer, Michael Lydon – Booth would not only be an observer, but
would himself become one of the characters in the great drama
that was unfolding and that is preserved in *Gimme Shelter*: one of
the observed.²² This was all new.

It seems clear that the idea that the Stones were 'the greatest
rock and roll band in the world' was derived from the infamy they
carried before them, already in 1969, and which would only become
greater. It is this 'greatness'– the excesses, the disregard for limits
on behaviour or movement, the freewheeling bohemianism – that
largely accounts for the continuing appeal of the Stones as the
ultimate survivors from an era during which so many fell by the
wayside or simply faded from public view, unable to cope with
the rigours of the road, the life of a rootless musician.

Within all of this, Booth's *The True Adventures of The Rolling
Stones* is the most singular chronicle of life on the road that
emerged from that era. But here was an individual who seemed
to possess the name of someone unsuited to the task – *Stanley
Booth*. Where 'Mick Jagger', by contrast, and as Booth himself
noted, had a name befitting of his rock 'n' roll persona – *Jagger*,
'a name to open sardine tins with', a name suitable to match
a haphazard existence, perhaps – his own handle suggested
something quite contrary to the person he actually was.²³ It
sounds like the name of an unassuming clerical officer from
Stevenage, or some other provincial outpost – English, reserved.
Stanley Booth – it doesn't sound very rock 'n' roll, but the truth
is that Booth himself was a pioneer: one of the first of his
generation driven by a need to be a part of this travelling circus,
who was barely motivated by the fact that it was a job that would
provide money to send back home to his partner. It was much
more than that – it's a cliché, but he saw that these five English
guys and their various hangers-on were taking the music he loved

and spearheading a change in the consciousness of the times. Writers like Booth not only reported on the transformation of popular music and its culture towards the end of the 1960s, but were themselves a part of that culture, 'participant observers' of a kind that no longer exist. The inside flap of *True Adventures* offers a short biography that reveals what might be credentials for this unlikely role for which there was no specialist training, and – actually – no credentials that could be obtained by any respectable means, or any kind of schooling in the conventional sense: he had previously worked as 'a karate teacher, a State welfare worker, a Pinkerton operative, and a writing teacher'. Here was a man like the Stones themselves in spirit; a man of inconsistent purpose, a writer who would hitch himself to this carnival in the hope of finding the truth that might allow him to make sense of this thing that American blues, rock 'n' roll and R&B had become since the days when he was writing of his encounters with the original performers he could find.

True Adventures is a tremendously evocative portrait of the end of the 1960s, a decade whose demise (in the form of the evident eclipse of its earlier idealism) has been closely associated with The Rolling Stones' infamous appearance at the Altamont Speedway in the last days of 1969, which was captured in some detail in *Gimme Shelter*. Both the book and the film (much more than later books and testimonies) attain a kind of timeless quality because they are a reminder that while the songs of any period on their own may have the power to evoke thoughts of the times and places that a listener lived through, or that a prospective listener might at some point want to revisit, it is the portraits of how the musicians who created these songs existed *in* those times and places – portraits in word and image – and the knowledge they provide of the deeds, the details and the seemingly superfluous cultural flotsam and jetsam, that ends up making a contribution to a more general kind of cultural memory of the period. *True*

Adventures, in particular, is also a remarkable document because of the sense that what one is reading is the very atmosphere of those times, which means that the willing reader is able to find a way inside the self-contained bubble around the musicians that would grow larger and more insulated from reality as the decades unfolded, and the sort of lengths that a band had to go to in order to make the music live – to live the music – and to become as one with its sentiments, became more determined.

In the case of the Stones, they seemed merely to be living up to their own name, borrowed from a Muddy Waters song, 'Rollin' Stone', whose subject, of course, was the lure of movement and travel.

If the Stones wanted their own mythographer, then they had found a writer whose own ambitions were to communicate life in a world that was always on the verge of falling apart in such a way that future generations would know what it was. 'I tried as consciously as I was able to write a book about famous people as if they were unknown to the reader,' Booth wrote in 1999, 'so that a hundred years later, say, someone could pick up the book and read it simply for the story, the working out of the character's destinies.'[24]

Booth's hunch was that the destinies of the Stones were altered forever by the mysterious death of founder member Brian Jones, who by the time of his departure from the band mere months before he was found floating in his swimming pool, was already a marginal figure who had taken a secondary role to that of Jagger and Richards. One of the most memorable chapters in *True Adventures* recounts Stanley Booth's own road trip to Cheltenham to try and find out more about the motivations of the band members, where he interviewed Jones's parents not long after his death. And there they were: two respectable middle-class people, probably born in the distant 1910s or 1920s, baffled by how this thing, 'rock 'n' roll', could forever have changed their polite

son from an aspiring draughtsman into the embodiment of
rock 'n' roll decadence.

Cheltenham, Gloucestershire, for Booth – who was from
the swamp country of Waycross, Georgia – was a foreign land.
So, of course, he recorded the kind of details that only a traveller
would latch onto – the fact that the only soft drink his hotel served
was orange squash seems strangely characteristic of how little
England ('Little England' he might have said), beyond its few
metropolitan centres, had changed in the previous twenty or 30
years. Is it any wonder that a Brian Jones or Keith Richards (or
a generation of British musicians) would become enamoured of
the vast United States, a land of plenty and opportunity; the place
where the only music that mattered to them permeated the very
air that ordinary people were able to breathe? But Cheltenham
nonetheless reminded Booth, he wrote, of Macon, Georgia,
where he went to school 'wearing an army uniform, carrying
a rifle': a conservative world.[25]

The True Adventures of The Rolling Stones was published some
fifteen years after the events it recounts took place. Stanley Booth
was there at Altamont, he carried Richards's guitar onstage, was
standing behind his amplifiers as the band played, and was the last
man scrambling onto the helicopter that the terrified band and a
few members of its entourage fled to after a performance that
had continued in the unspoken hope that a bad situation with
no apparent way out might not get any worse:

> We saw [Hells] Angels hitting people over the head with
> lead-weighted pool cues, using them like baseball bats. After
> Meredith [Hunter] died the Stones played for another hour-
> and-a-half and they played a brilliant, brilliant show. It was an
> heroic performance. At that point we assumed that several
> people had died. We saw so many people knocked down and
> pounded upon.[26]

Scenes from *Gimme Shelter*, filmed at Altamont Speedway. Fans arriving in good spirits (top), and a member of the Hell's Angels wielding a pool cue beats up members of the audience (bottom).

Booth's proximity to his subject shows in the way that the story of that time is told, more than a decade after he left the Stones behind, and after he had plenty of time to reflect on the experience and draw on the person that he had become by what then seemed the very distant 1980s. It is little surprise that later editions of the book bear the stamp of approval of the individual who most came to embody the identification of The Rolling Stones with the rock 'n' roll lifestyle, Keith Richards, whose words grace the cover: 'Stanley Booth's book is the only one I can read and say, "Yeah, that's how it was."'

But this is no censored, 'official' biography. The portrait
it paints is often unflattering. Of first meeting Keith Richards,
for instance, Booth describes seeing in the guitarist 'an insane
advertisement for dangerous carefree death':

> Black ragged hair, dead green skin, a cougar tooth hanging
> from his right earlobe, his lips snarled back from the
> marijuana cigarette between his rotting fangs.[27]

And in light of all that has been said about Altamont – the death
of the 'peace and love' optimism of the '60s – what more could be
said about it, especially by a first-hand witness who had stood at
the side of the stage as the Stones performed? *True Adventures* was
first published fifteen years after Altamont – and in the time that
had elapsed between the events and the publication of Booth's
book, countless others (including many who weren't witnesses
to the event) had taken turns to tell the story. But you know from
the opening paragraph of *True Adventures*, which takes place as
Jagger, Richards and Booth make a visit to the site of the gig the
night before, riding in a car through the darkness and in search
of this unlikely venue for a concert out in the middle of nowhere
– Altamont Speedway – that it is the sense of a place and its
atmosphere that ends up transforming the culture of this music
from something mundane into the carrier of cultural memory:

> It is late. All the little snakes are asleep. The world is black
> outside the car windows, just the dusty clay road in the
> headlights. Far from the city, past the last crossroads (where
> they used to bury suicides in England, with wooden stakes
> driven through their hearts), we are looking for a strange
> California hillside where we may see him, may even dance
> with him in his torn, bloody skins, come and play.[28]

That last sentence probably inspired the original publisher's preferred title, 'Dance with the Devil'– and perhaps refers to how apt the Stones' own 'Sympathy for the Devil' would be in soundtracking their own 1969. Booth's recollections are brimming with the sense that The Rolling Stones had created, or allowed to develop around them, a dangerous kind of weather. The best way to avoid it was to steer clear. 'In Keith's sitting room', Stanley wrote, 'we had cocaine and Old Charter for breakfast, swapped addresses and suddenly it was over.'[29]

LIVER THAN YOU'LL EVER BE

What remained when the touring was over, as the Stones knew, were the documents – the dispatches penned by the assorted writers who had temporarily joined the entourage as it cut a path across America, the photographs, the films and the other souvenirs picked up along the way. But there was also, by the late 1960s, a different kind of souvenir aimed more at the committed fan than the performer returning from tour – live recordings of concert performances that, at their best, often captured the essence of what it was that motivated the performers to take up their instruments in the first place. These bootlegs, made illicitly and distributed illegally, presented the sound of a phenomenon more immediate, and perhaps more real, than the studio artefacts that – no matter how vital and emotionally true they might be, no matter how filled with abandon and even menace – were a different kind of thing.

The Stones of 1969 provided the occasion for one of the first live bootleg albums to become widely available and achieve a relative measure of success – the excellent *LiveR than You'll Ever Be*, recorded in Oakland, California, on 9 November 1969 by an enterprising bootlegger named Dub. It was famously hailed by Greil Marcus at the time as the greatest album the Stones had ever made. The bootlegger, the so-called 'Dub' (a term that means 'copy' in recording parlance), was interested in releasing quality products, and had travelled around the United States on the tour in search of the best results, capturing 'performances with a two-track Sony tape recorder', which was probably the best equipment that could be smuggled unnoticed into concert venues at the time.[30] Estimates of the sales of this record in an article in the trade magazine *Billboard* in 1970 – now viewed as probably over-estimated – gave a figure of 250,000 copies, more than half of which were reputedly bootlegs of the original bootleg.[31] By the early 1970s there had been a huge growth in the demand and production of these recordings which, in tune with the times, were 'an artifact of the alternative lifestyle', which gained exposure through the most influential organs of the alternative media, and eventually in magazines that existed somewhere between alternative and mainstream, such as *Rolling Stone*, which ended up reviewing bootlegs alongside official releases.[32] Within a few years, other more advanced bootleggers would be utilizing 'microphones with in-built FM radio transmitters' that were able to 'broadcast directly from the concert', sending their signals to a vehicle kitted out with recording equipment that was parked just outside the concert venue.[33]

LiveR than You'll Ever Be came to be regarded as an indispensible document of the Stones at the peak of their performing powers, and – some said – was a recording of such good quality that it couldn't possibly have been recorded without the collusion of the band themselves. But it was soon enough revealed to be the genuine product of a lone bootlegger, who just happened to find almost the perfect spot in the Oakland arena from where his microphone was able to capture something of the essence of how the performance actually sounded to those present.[34] Because of the success of *LiveR*, the band's record company was pushed into releasing an official document of the Stones on that tour, the acclaimed *Get Yer Ya-Ya's Out!*, to counter the momentum that bootleggers seemed to be enjoying. It was even admitted later by those who had released the Stones bootleg that the Mafia had been interested in bringing their distribution skills into play to get an angle on this new facet of the music business (they had already been involved in running factories that produced counterfeit copies of official albums).[35]

Official live releases, of course, benefited from the fact that they were widely distributed and easy to find in stores – and because of that, the effect of *LiveR than You'll Ever Be* was not to soak up sales that would otherwise have gone to The Rolling Stones' record company, but rather to stoke up interest in the official release, ensuring that when it was released it was still a best-seller.

7 LIVE IN FRONT OF YOUR NAKED EYES AND EARS

BLASTING, SCREAMING AND STOMPING

Despite the quality of the performances on The Rolling Stones' official live document of their 1969 tour, *Get Yer Ya-Ya's Out!*, and its sonic superiority, it nonetheless – and strangely, perhaps – could not match the spark and the air of vitality that *LiveR than You'll Ever Be* had captured; perhaps due to the inevitable studio polishing and mixing that was a part of the official recording's journey from performance to record.

Regardless of the relative merits of the sound quality, those extra stages of 'processing' ensured that it could not convey the sense of being a primary document of the event that had, due to some good fortune, been snatched as a moment in time. It was *that* quality that became the kind of aura that even the most amateurishly recorded bootleg releases were able to acquire for the discerning collector. And, as Clinton Heylin wrote, The Rolling Stones were quite happy that the bootleg was out there anyway, and even for people to think that they had something to do with a release that represented an attack on the commercial endeavours of their record company – they were the rock 'n' roll outlaws, after all:

If there was ever any real evidence implicating the Stones in the production of *LiveR Than You'll Ever Be*, they did not go out of their way to condemn the release. When some copies were brought up to KSAN radio station in San Francisco, Sam

Cutler, the Stones' road manager, listened to it and ended up buying six copies, one for himself, the remaining five for the Stones themselves.[1]

Some bootlegs, like that of Bob Dylan's concert at the Manchester Free Trade Hall in 1966 (long believed to have been recorded at the Royal Albert Hall in London) took on legendary status as genuine historical artefacts that captured moments that were representative of wider and more seismic cultural upheavals.

In the case of the supposed 'Royal Albert Hall' bootleg, the moment that was preserved was much more than just a musical performance of an artist following a new path; it was the point at which the will of an artist was brought into direct confrontation with the expectations of his audience, resulting in a symbolic and decisive assertion of creative independence. The 'Royal Albert Hall' concert of 1966, for as long as it had existed on bootleg, had gone down in legend as the event when a member of the audience shouted 'Judas' at Bob Dylan as he was tuning up between songs – for having the nerve to appear onstage with an electric rock 'n' roll backing band. These kind of catcalls had been in the air for some time at Dylan concerts, and had started at the Newport Folk Festival in 1965, that 'most sacred of folk events', as Lee Marshall describes it, when Dylan most publicly seemed to turn against the folk revival that had carried him to his early prominence.[2]

So, what happened that night in England was the culmination of over a year's worth of audience heckling in the United States, and anywhere else he had played to an audience with his new electric backing band. But the two-part nature of his concerts at the time – half acoustic and half electric – revealed that it was noise and amplification that was at the root of the problem. Dylan would first play a solo set, giving performances that 'were well received':

After a break he would return supported by The Band and play an electric set culminating in 'Like a Rolling Stone.' Everywhere Dylan played these electrified performances were booed by the audience and Dylan argued with hecklers.[3]

These concerts, Marshall argues, assumed the aura of myth-like confrontations in accounts of Dylan's evolving artistry, aided by the evidence of this bootleg in particular, which itself took on the status of some kind of archaeological oracle foretelling the many future departures from expectation that would become almost his chief artistic characteristic.

What agitated audiences in 1965–6 arguably had much to do with the air of nonchalant enthusiasm that the leather-jacketed Dylan, often seen in dark sunglasses, evidently gave off in his purposeful dismantling of the folk persona that had seemed to define him for these audiences. But the thing about electric rock music was not just that it was some variety of rock 'n' roll music (rather than the so-called folk music that fired the hearts of so many at that time). To be sure, within the context of the ethos of political activism that marked the folk revival, his embrace of amplification – the electric guitars and drums were instruments of noise to many – cancelled out the purity of the 'message', or sentiments that song at its purest was supposed to provide access to. So while on the one hand the amplification provided evidence of how compromised Dylan had become by his own success and how driven he seemed to be in pursuing further commercial success, on the other hand, the violence of that noise symbolized the severing of the connection that existed between the song and the listener that his presence was meant to ensure; instead, his voice was technologically mediated and engulfed by the excessive volume of the now further amplified and projected sound.

Amplification provides a different kind of *transmission* to the more or less unadorned voice. The latter comes close to the folk ideal of communication, which would be direct, unmediated and characteristic, so to speak, of face-to-face relations. In that context, the performance of song is, like other sounds that are authentic, 'bound by the unity of experience, sentiment and place'.[4] But in the case of a musical phenomenon like the folk revival, Dylan surely knew that this idealized relationship was already a chimera, and that the folk revival was already defined in part by the successes of its own recording stars, who existed within the so-called 'audio-industrial complex'.[5] Those of Bob Dylan's records that had found favour with his earliest fans were, in an important sense, already 'amplified' – they had made his presence into something that was more than the flesh and bones Robert Zimmerman; newly enlarged, expanded and capable of being communicated via technological means to times and places entirely unconnected with the performances that made up his body of recorded work.

As Paul Hegarty notes in his history of noise in music, 'phonograph and gramophone technology is entirely bound up with amplification', and as such is a separate entity from the source that is captured in recording.[6] In a sense, it floats free from its source to become what the philosopher Friedrich Kittler described as a kind of 'weightless matter', at once released from its source yet inscribed in some form (on cylinders, records, tapes and so on) that allows it to travel and to communicate far and wide.[7]

The moment of the 'Judas' taunt also later emerged on film, in Martin Scorsese's documentary about Bob Dylan, *No Direction Home* (2005), which revealed previously unseen footage of the event and captured the anger of fans exiting the concert in disgust at this 'rubbish' – this 'pop band backing' – that was drowning out Dylan's words. But as the cry of 'Judas' hung in the air, the visibly angry Dylan drawled back to the accuser: 'I don't be-*leeeeive* you. You're a liar'. He turned defiantly towards his backing musicians, The Hawks (who later became famous in their own right as The

Band), with a few simple and direct words that revealed his intention to continue as he pleased: 'play fucking loud', he told them.

When this performance found an official release decades later, and by then correctly identified as the 1966 concert at Manchester's Free Trade Hall, it was as part of Dylan's own official *Bootleg Series* with Columbia Records. And despite the recording of the concert coming in this case from an official rather than audience source, it had not been diminished in its power by the passing of time. It's toughness and 'sustained intensity', Anthony Varesi said, made it 'the maddest, most majestic music Bob Dylan – or anyone else – ever made'.[8] It had, probably more than any other official live recording that was released from recordings made in the 1960s and '70s, acquired the status of genuine historical artefact.

There were other notable documents of this kind, which captured either rock 'n' roll or particularly notable figures in its history, in some moment of transformation. The Beatles' *Live! at the Star-Club in Hamburg, Germany; 1962* was a concert recorded in December of that year on a reel-to-reel recorder by a British musician – Ted Taylor of Kingsize Taylor and the Dominoes – who, like The Beatles, was performing in Hamburg at the time. It provides the clearest evidence of what they were like in the final months before they were transformed into an entirely different phenomenon – the source of Beatlemania – that soon took the world by storm. The recording was lost for some ten years, and not released until fifteen years after it was recorded; long enough to ensure that it was akin to an archaeological discovery that shattered the hitherto-existing perception of The Beatles as four aging hangovers from another age who had often seemed to venture a bit too much into middle-of-the-road territory as solo performers. But here, in this distinctly low-fi document, was something that sounded like a throwback to a prehistoric rock 'n' roll era, where The Beatles were as direct and aggressive as the most uncompromising rock music of the time tried to be. As the remnant of a time that seemed to be undocumented, it 'arrived with the suddenness of suppressed memory' and seemed to be perfectly in tune with the ethos and sound of the punk bands of 1977, its year of release.[9] There was something 'clear and evident' about the performances on this Star-Club recording that made the album more real than the representations of The Beatles that were very familiar to the public at large. It was not 'just music', Devin McKinney wrote; it was:

> the sound of deep emotional experience pressed into the tightest, most intense space imaginable. In other words, it is something like life. Not a scrap of life or a stolen glance at life as in most pop music – a moment's epiphany of connection to a cosmic oneness. Heard as a whole, the Beatles' last Hamburg performance is a large, weighty chunk of real existence.[10]

The connection to the real, and the pursuit of authenticity, is what marks so many of the live albums that would arrive in a flood during the 1970s. An industry report on the phenomenon for *Billboard* in 1974 declared that it was one of the major trends in the music world, and that it 'was not uncommon now to find between fifteen and twenty live albums on the charts at any given time'.[11] These products may have served the function for the record companies of being cheap options which, in the service of easy profits, they were eager to keep on knocking out, but they were more than that. It is true that the record companies had, as a by-product of trying to counter live concert bootlegs, hit on a most profitable formula: here was a product with minimal recording costs attached to it, and with the high consumer appeal of track listings usually composed of well-known songs, and so likely to be popular with buyers. But it was an era when these releases also worked to the artists' advantage, because they offered a vehicle through which musicians felt they could express their connection to the real nitty-gritty of their existence as a road band. Just look at the titles of some of these albums – *Live and Dangerous, Kick Out the Jams, On Your Feet or On Your Knees, It's Alive, Rock 'n' roll Animal, Undead*. As the recording manager for the most successful mobile recording unit of the era, Wally Heider Recording of San Francisco, said at the time, the musicians were – by the turn of the 1970s – much better players than they had been before, 'particularly those that had been around a while and perfected their stage show'.[12] And one particular appeal of the live album for performers and consumers alike was the sound of 'the feedback and energy from the audience' that came over on the best of these recordings.[13] To get the 'live' version of your favourite band was to get the most in-your-face, uncompromising and raw version – the truest apparent representation, which is one reason why the sound of the audience on these albums is so important; it testified to the excitement and aliveness of it all.

Live albums would also be the route through which younger audiences were introduced to the older American forms – particularly the blues – that had such a formative influence on the white rock bands of the 1960s and '70s. The albums captured what otherwise would not exist apart from in the moment of performance. So, where the first-hand experience of young listeners to these bands who paid homage to their deeper influences onstage might offer some kind of glimpse of these influences, it was more of a peek-a-boo – it was still only a snatch of something that vanished into the ether as soon as it was over, and you might never know what it was. These influences, though, became more important as soon as they were 'documented' – that is, recorded – in a form that could be revisited with the kind of attention that repeated listening allows.

Those old blues songs, which in many cases were played onstage to expand the performance over longer and longer set times, were often little more than blueprints for onstage exercises in stretching, bending and re-forming a song that might have been only two or three minutes long in its original version. They became something quite different to the source material, but nonetheless important in opening the way to the discovery of a musical past that contained seemingly unlimited riches from times that predated rock 'n' roll. As Robert Santelli recalled, for listeners who saw names like Robert Johnson and Sonny Boy Williamson attached to the contemporary artists they looked up to, 'every day seemed to bring a new revelation', an opportunity to 'venture back in time'.[14] Almost every significant performer of the era that elevated live performance to a status at least the equal of records – The Doors, Janis Joplin, Jimi Hendrix, The Rolling Stones and Led Zeppelin – were a route to the roots of this phenomenon in 'blues, folk, and then early country, jazz, gospel, and every other pre-rock sound that helped determine America's musical identity in the twentieth century'.[15]

One of the most notable and influential examples of how these old blues songs functioned as blueprints for explorations in performance was the British trio Cream's live recording of 'Crossroads' in 1968 – their take on Robert Johnson's 'Cross Road Blues' (and incorporating lines from another song, 'Traveling Riverside Blues'), which extends from the recognizable lyric of the opening verses into a long instrumental workout that was more akin to what one would expect from jazz – with Eric Clapton reaching a plane of instrumental expression that could sit alongside any soloist from that genre – and helped to seal Cream's reputation as one of the most inspired live acts of the late 1960s. In a similar fashion, the Allman Brothers took 'One Way Out', an old blues song by Sonny Boy Williamson, and transformed it into an expression of the kind of unbounded ecstasy that could move both player and listener into an entirely new space of experience. In both of those examples it would be difficult to imagine them existing as the outcome of studio performances, so palpable is the sense of event and the interaction between the instrumentalists in the band – playing off each other and moving in directions that were spontaneous and unexpected – and between the band and the audience.

Sound recording, no matter what its object, had always allowed what were akin to fragments of time and reality to be preserved, in ways that not only served as a means for the transmission of the kind of 'atmosphere' that defined times, places or events, but that could also alter or adjust our perception of that reality, by adding depth and substance to it.[16] In the case of such official live recordings of concert performances, the ostensible aim – in artistic terms – was to produce something that provided a connection to the moment of performance: to the singular *event* of performance, as something that was an essentially unrepeatable phenomenon. For the listener, these albums were sold as something that was as close to actually being there – in the absence of a time machine – as possible.

LIVING IN AMERICA

If nothing else, live recordings – including both bootlegs and officially sanctioned albums – were indicators of the new importance that was attached to prolonged periods of touring. They also signalled a new and expanding culture around rock music, the rise of vinyl artefacts that, a few short years earlier, were almost non-existent outside jazz. During the 1970s, touring in America would be the way that countless musicians were able to take up residence in this new and shifting milieu. And while live performance and multi-date touring of a kind had a long history, much had changed by the late 1960s. The impact of these changes would be to put the artists – especially the successful ones – more firmly in control than they had ever been before.

One early precursor of modern touring that also reflected how much travel had become part of the musician's way of life, was the travelling medicine shows of the early twentieth century, which featured a motley collection of performers (musicians, jugglers, salesmen). By the time Hank Williams, for instance, had recorded his first major-label singles for MGM in 1948, he had already spent significant time on the road, performing in travelling medicine shows that criss-crossed the South selling elixirs that were laced with alcohol at a time (and in places) where alcohol was hard to come by. The music, of course, was of secondary importance. Muddy Waters, too, sometimes played with travelling medicine shows that passed through Mississippi, although he never actually went on the road with them.

Elsewhere, in the 1940s and '50s, black musicians were often only able to tour through a segregated United States on the 'chitlin' circuit' – 'a string of black-owned honky-tonks, night clubs, and theaters' – so-called because the venues also served up chitlins (chitterlings) and other soul food.[17] In that pre-civil rights era, this circuit sustained the careers of performers such as James Brown, B.B. King, Ray Charles and Aretha Franklin. They played often in revues alongside cabaret acts, dancers and comedians. But it provided the main means of honing the well-rehearsed stage acts that more general audiences saw occasionally on television, and would come to hear on breakthrough records, like James Brown's landmark release in 1963, *Live at the Apollo*. In fact, Brown's commitment to performing as a means towards the end of eventually carving out a space for artistic freedom – that found expression on his self-produced records of the 1960s and '70s – was so total as to include appearing as someone else in order to earn money.

Thus it was that, in 1955, James Brown appeared *as* Little Richard – not merely in place of him – after the chart success of 'Tutti Frutti' had lured Richard to California to record a follow-up. 'Brown toured with Richard's band, The Upsetters', Preston Lauterbach wrote, 'and traveled in the station wagon the band used, emblazoned with Little Richard's name and song titles'.[18] In those venues, which were mainly spread across the South and the Midwest – and found in cities like Detroit, Macon, Houston, Memphis and New Orleans – apprenticeships were served, and faltering careers found a new direction. It was on the chitlin' circuit that Jimi Hendrix, for instance, cut his teeth playing as a sideman for acts like The Isley Brothers and Little Richard, whose star was somewhat in decline by the early to mid-1960s. As Frederick Opie notes, the roadwork involved was punishing:

> Performers would often do consecutive one-night stands, frequently more than eight-hundred miles apart. The routine went: drive for hours, stop, set-up the bandstand, play for five hours, break down the bandstand, and drive for several more hours. On the road, performers often settled for sandwiches from the colored window of segregated restaurants until they arrived at the next venue.[19]

The years spent on the chitlin' circuit helped James Brown, who had acquired a formidable reputation as a live performer and built up a huge following, performing over 300 shows a year, justify his self-proclaimed title of The Hardest-Working Man in Show Business. But the chitlin' circuit was almost a closed world, set apart from the mainstream – that is, white – pop world that Brown knew he could break, if only it could hear him. 'A few hip whites came, but not many', he recalled of the days on the chitlin' circuit:

I remember one young man, a white kid, who slipped backstage at a gig in Florida in 1959 when I was still scuffling. He knew everything on the 'Please' album. I couldn't believe it.[20]

Live at the Apollo was recorded at the legendary Apollo Theater in Harlem, which at that time represented 'the tar paper ceiling of the chitlin' circuit' – which is to say that once you reached there, there was nowhere else to go but to find a way to break out into the mainstream, which was exactly what the live album would manage to achieve.[21] The recording, at just over 30 minutes in length, not only documents the Godfather of Soul at the peak of his performing powers, but in capturing the interplay of audience and performer on an evening of high excitement, it was a precursor to the live rock albums of the 1970s which attempted to preserve the fizz and electricity of a performance space brought to life in a unique kind of temporary collective experience.

Live at the Apollo begins with the relatively calm voice of the MC, Fats Gonder – 'Good evening, ladies and gentlemen. Are you ready for star time?' – which, in short order, becomes a performance all on its own, full of rhythm and cadence and the rhetorical skills of the committed preacher who is able to toy with attentive listeners running high on anticipation:

Thank you and thank you very kindly. It's indeed a great pleasure to present to you at this particular time, nationally and internationally known as the Hardest-Working Man in Show Business . . .

As the MC proceeds to run off a list of Brown's hits, one after another, the band stabs out a collective chord, and the audience screams each time in response:

the man who sings 'I'll Go Crazy'! . . . 'Try *ME*'! . . .
'*YOU've* Got the Power'! . . . '*Think*'!! . . . 'If You Want Me'!
. . . 'I Don't Mind' . . . '*BE-wild-ered*'!!

Higher and higher up the musical scale the band go, and the
louder and more insistent the horn stabs (and screams) become,
until it sounds like the temperature of the room has been blown-
up to bursting point:

Million-dollar seller – '*Lost Someone*'!! . . . The very latest
release, '*Night Train*'!! . . . Let's everybody 'Shout and
SHIMMY'!! . . . Mr Dynamite, the amazing Mr Please Please
himself, the star of the show, *James Brown and the Famous
Flames*!

The Famous Flames then burst into a quick rhythm and blues
vamp, with a fast-driving guitar and more repeated horn stabs –
it's like the sound of a train, all horns blazing, coming right at
the audience – continuing to raise the temperature of the room.
As James Brown finally hits the stage, a mere minute and a half
after Fats Gonder opened his mouth to utter those first words,
the audience – by this point loudly gasping and screaming –
seems to have almost lost control of itself. And the sense of
frenzy doesn't let up. The band launches into one of Brown's
biggest hits, 'I'll Go Crazy' – *if you leave me, I'll go crazy*, he sings
repeatedly – that leaves the audience screaming ecstatically at
every refrain of the line, which they are now convinced is a plea
directed to each one of them in that room, on that night, and to
no one else. It is a demonstration of supreme stagecraft, which
opens up into an exchange of energy that feeds the performers
and audience alike, making it truly an event, a co-existence of
players – musicians and spectators – who have come together and
exist, for the briefest of periods, totally in sync with each other.

James Brown broke out of the chitlin' circuit by assuming total control over his own career – packaging his own shows, producing his own records and buying radio stations, which at the time were overwhelmingly white-owned; even those that played black music.[22] It was, as Jerry Butler – a fellow chitlin' circuit veteran – observed, in 'rebellion against the kind of "plantation" atmosphere that permeated the entertainment industry' at the time.[23] The *Live at the Apollo* album was a gamble Brown took on his own – paying for the recording costs out of his own pocket and hiring out the theatre for a week's worth of shows – and it paid off.[24] No one at the time was interested in live albums, but it capitalized on Brown's great strength as a performer and heralded something new; 'so staggeringly new it scarcely bore any connection to the music *called* rhythm and blues'.[25] It became the fastest selling album of his career, reaching number two on the mainstream pop albums chart and remaining there for over a year.

As far as road music goes, Brown's number one hit single of the 1980s, 'Living in America', with its evocation of the 'all night diners that keep you awake', the 'motels' and 'many miles of railroad track', is a perfect example. Although written for Brown by other songwriters, it reflected his life and early experience of America when he was almost constantly on the road as a performer.[26]

Beyond the chitlin' circuit, however, there was no real infrastructure for touring nationally that could accommodate the new rock culture, which produced the biggest ever boom in popular music history – not until the late 1960s did a new environment begin to take shape. It took a number of developments, the long-standing impacts of which have not often been assessed in terms of their importance – such as the emergence of the new kind of audience that The Rolling Stones first encountered on their 1969 tour, a commitment to improving the presentation of live shows, and the development of improvements in amplification for projecting the sound of a band on a small stage out to audiences that were growing larger and more discerning than the screaming teenagers of just a few years previously. What cannot be doubted is that the music that had inflamed the hearts and inspired the dreams of millions of teenagers in the 1950s and early '60s had been the kind of pop music that was to be found on the Top 40 charts. When translated into a live performance context, it could be seen in touring revues that were more like variety shows, and, by contrast to the situation that would develop in the 1970s, designed to make more money for promoters than artists. The kind of billing which featured – usually – a headliner with an opening act or two, would not become the norm until the late 1960s and '70s. Given the importance of regional markets in radio in the United States at the time, these kinds of Top 40 revues, which traversed the country playing state fairs and movie theatres, usually involved a mix of performers. Performers who were on the national charts played alongside popular regional acts, and all – even the stars of the show – played a mere handful of songs. If nothing else, these kind of tours served to make budding artists realize they were no more than the filling in a superficial musical entertainment showcase served up to satisfy a primarily teenage audience. Artistry had little to do with it. This was illustrated in the film *That Thing You Do!* (1996), which characterized the early '60s era as one where the performers were wholly powerless over how their music was presented in a live setting.

On their first tours of the u.s., British bands like The Rolling Stones and The Yardbirds gained valuable exposure performing as part of such package tours, which had been a fixture in the lives of countless performers since the rise of rock 'n' roll in the mid-1950s. But the technological limitations of the often improvised venues, which had sprung up to meet the growing demand for live performances, were exposed during The Beatles' final tour of the

The Beatles at Shea Stadium, New York, 1965.

u.s. In photographs and newsreel footage of some of these concerts it seems almost as if the band were the victims of some cruel joke perpetrated by shameless promoters who were merely out to fleece the young audience. There, for all to see (if not to hear, as it turned out), the four tiny figures of The Beatles stood on a little rectangular stage facing a sports stadium filled to the gills with screaming fans, with only the sound of their little Vox AC30 amplifiers and the perfunctory public address systems there to project the sound they made onstage. This, more than anything else, was the reason that The Beatles retired from live performance in 1966 – their concerts had become, John Lennon remarked, 'just bloody tribal rituals'.[27] Not only had they advanced as a recording band, becoming much more self-conscious about being artists (rather than teen pop fodder), but there was simply not the technology, the infrastructure or logistics to manage performances for such large audiences. What happened in 1966 on these u.s. dates repeated their experience of the previous year, when they had set a new concert attendance record at Shea Stadium in New York. The sense of the event itself having overtaken the music was evident in the hysterical audience reaction to a helicopter that appeared, at one point, above the stadium. It became 'an object of intense scrutiny, a symbol of the event waiting to happen [if not] the audience's desire to immerse themselves in the event'.[28] It was a scene recreated in *A Star is Born* (1975), co-scripted by Joan Didion, when Kris Kristofferson and Barbra Streisand – a rock star in the Jim Morrison mould and his girlfriend – hover over Sun Devil Stadium whipping up excitement in the audience below as one of the opening acts, a real band named Montrose, played onstage. The scene provided an easy means of signifying the new mass appeal of rock music.

Within two or three years of The Beatles' final concert at Candlestick Park in San Francisco, however, rock music moved into a period of rapid changes, propelled by better amplification and PA systems suitable for basketball game-sized arenas and outdoor stadiums, and, not least, the arrival of a generation of performers who were willing to put up with the drudgery of life on tour, especially – in the case of the British bands who would be the pioneers of these intense jaunts across America – as they were able to see the birthplace of the blues and rock 'n' roll at first hand. What these British bands did, in a sense, was to colonize the country, establishing the itinerary of the rock tour for the next decade, all while promoting a version of the authentic life that came out of the influence of generations of American musicians going back to the Delta blues. Because they were foreigners, the only way to become American, so to speak, was to immerse themselves as fully as possible in the myths of the blues and rock 'n' roll. To be a real and uncompromising musician, it seemed, meant giving oneself over to the road and living and breathing the life it entailed; a life of constant movement. In that kind of commitment was the ideal of unfettered personal and musical freedom that was so in tune with the times.

ROADWORK

The ascendance of the on-the-road culture had everything to do with the changing nature of how rock music was experienced. As a form of mass entertainment, driven by records and radio, popular music certainly changed in its relationship to its audience – in step with technological developments, but also as the culture, more generally, was transformed by non-musical social forces in the 1970s. During the 1950s, rock music – as a *visual* experience – was seen mostly on the television and not in person; and often, indeed, as a partial representation (as was the case with the early broadcasts of Elvis Presley, whose below-the-waist gyrating was censored). Television was arguably the only visual contact for most of those fans who were buying the records and listening to the music on the radio. But this gradually changed in the 1960s as concerts started to rival TV as a means of actually experiencing the visual aspect of a musical performance, something that was entrenched further in the following decade.[29]

The key change was in the rise to prominence of a number of powerful promoters whose influence rested on the relationships they had forged with touring bands (and their managers), often by guaranteeing ticket sales in the regional markets they controlled, which in turn made them work tirelessly to promote shows. One of the influential promoters of the era was Don Law, who ruled the concert scene in Boston during the late 1960s and early '70s, and was manager of the most influential venue in New England, The Boston Tea Party. It was performances there that had helped to break British bands such as Fleetwood Mac, Ten Years After and Led Zeppelin in the United States. And like those bands, he had a connection to the Delta blues – in his case it was through his father, the *other* Don Law; the producer with Columbia Records who, back in 1936, had recorded those seminal Robert Johnson sides in San Antonio, Texas.

Some of the new players would end up with much larger empires than the mainly local and regional fiefdoms of players like Don Law in Boston, or Bill Graham in New York and San Francisco, and became hugely influential on the careers of the performers they handled. The most significant of these figures was Frank Barsalona, who established the Premier Talent Agency in 1964. Prior to this, he had spent some time working as a booking agent for the General Artists Corporation (or GAC), which had a long history in show business but no real interest in the rock bands they handled. The screaming teenage girls and the novelty of the succession of British Invasion bands that followed on the heels of The Beatles seemed to be part of some kind of fad, rather than the emergence of anything that might last. Frank Barsalona 'discovered that it was easy to sign rock acts, hard to book them, and impossible to sustain their careers'.[30] But by the turn of the 1970s his company, Premier, had become the most influential booking agency in the country and – the way he told it – dragged the concert promotion business ('the asshole of show business') from a position akin to rodeo shows into an enterprise that had real clout, and which raised the bar for live performances, making concerts as important as records to many artists' own perceptions of who they were and what they did.[31] 'One of the most important things about Premier', Barsalona explained,

> is that we developed the [regional] rock promoters as well. Unlike the agencies before, who went to the established promoters, we developed new promoters, young promoters . . . people who did nothing else but rock, and who knew the music, liked the music, heard about the music.[32]

Premier played a big part in the normalizing of the often gruelling u.s.-wide tours that bands of that era – British bands in particular, desperate to break into nationwide success – would undertake. One British band whose fortunes were turned around by their association with Premier was Humble Pie, a hard rock-blues outfit formed by ex-Small Faces singer Steve Marriott, and also featuring future '70s megastar Peter Frampton (once dismissed by the NME as a token 'pretty boy'). After a couple of flop albums in the UK, Humble Pie turned their attentions to the u.s., where their new harder rock direction was thought – especially in the wake of Led Zeppelin's success in 1969–70 – to stand a chance of breaking the band into the big time.

Humble Pie hooked up with one of the most ruthless managers in the business, Dee Anthony, who managed a raft of British acts in America. Because of his close relationship with Frank Barsalona – who acted on behalf of all his acts – Anthony hatched a plan to put Humble Pie 'on the road and keep them there' until their reputation as a live band was sealed, and then build on that exposure to break the charts.[33] It was no accident that English groups were able to have an impact on the back of their roadwork – the infrastructure for large-scale touring may not have been as well-developed as it would be in as little as five years' time, but the work permit restrictions placed on performers visiting the u.s. ended up making a major contribution to their eventual success. Short, well-organized and intense tours were planned with maximum exposure in all the important markets in mind. As Frank Barsalona said in 1970, because the English bands could only spend a total of a few months a year working in the United States, Premier had to 'book them in perhaps 26 or 27 markets for a one month tour'.[34] American bands, by contrast, would cover 'the same ground in four months', arguably making it more difficult to have the kind of immediate impact that successive waves of bands from the uk had.[35]

The key to using Premier and the repeated bouts of roadwork to batter a route into the charts, Anthony believed, was to capitalize on the new road-credibility gained through intensive touring to record a live concert album. It was a strategy he 'soon applied with great success to the careers of his three most important clients, J. Geils, Joe Cocker, and Humble Pie'.[36] The major markets in the u.s. and Canada were established on the basis of record sales and radio airplay in key cities, and the level of interest in Premier's roster of bands from local promoters requesting booking prices.[37] And in the case of Humble Pie, as drummer Jerry Shirley remembered, the band's gruelling months on the road were deliberately planned as the perfect preparations for a live album, allowing them to set the tapes rolling at the Fillmore in late May 1971, just as they had reached a peak of performance. 'As we were heading into the recording of the live album, we knew we were getting better and better, doing bigger and bigger shows . . . it was very magical. Everything was going right.'[38]

Wham! An advert for Humble Pie, *Performance: Rockin' the Fillmore*, 1972, suggests that on this occasion the earth did move.

It took Humble Pie a lot of hard work to make the breakthrough, and repeated visits to the areas where they were going down well. *Cash Box* magazine reported on earlier appearances at the Fillmore East on 19–20 March 1971, noting the 'staggering' stage performance and the group's 'musical abilities' – especially now that this had been coupled with 'the many considerations that go into the making of a rock group. Its members. Material. Management. Record label. Booking agent' – had put them in a position to become a 'major force in rock music'.[39] The breakthrough came, as predicted, with the release of the blistering live album, *Performance: Rockin' the Fillmore*, which had captured, as one advert for the album suggested, a performance that swept aside everything else they had ever done:

> Having slowly worked their way up from making $500 to $1,000 as the opening act on a Premier package tour, Humble Pie were now commanding between $3,500 and $5,000 a night. With the album's release, the group's guarantee immediately jumped to $10,000.[40]

While the promoters were rewarded for their efforts with generous percentages of the tour income, some of the musicians, especially the members of those bands further down the food chain opening for more established acts, often eked out the most basic existence on their tiny daily cash allowances (or 'per diems'). One of Dee Anthony's clients who tended to fill out the bill on the u.s. tours for his more well-known acts was the San Francisco hard-rock band Montrose, whose debut album of 1973 – also named *Montrose* – would ultimately go on to become a slow burn success (it took more than a decade to reach platinum sales in the u.s.) and a landmark album of the genre. But in the period between 1973 and 1975, Montrose were repeatedly forced out onto the road just to try and scrape a living. The pace of the touring, the lack of money – $150 dollars a week and $10 per band member as on-the-road expenses each day – and the fact that they were playing to audiences that were there for the headline acts, meant that they were little more than filler in the package. In the end, it was this sense of going round and round and getting nowhere that killed the band. 'We just went out to tour', recalled singer Sammy Hagar, 'and basically never came back.'[41] Anthony had Montrose opening, much of the time, for more established acts such as the J. Geils Band and Humble Pie, both of which seemed to be permanently on tour as well. The band did not go down that well, Hagar recalled:

> But we were working or traveling seven nights a week. Sometimes we'd even do a club the same night. We'd open for Humble Pie at the arena, then run over and do an eleven o'clock show at the club to make a little extra money . . . We were making $500 a night and it was costing about $600 a night to tour. We were dying.[42]

Ironically, when Hagar did begin to break in the mid- to late 1970s, it was on the back of the touring-to-live album formula established by Dee Anthony, with his solo release *All Night Long* (1978), a re-presentation of many of the songs that he wrote for and recorded with Montrose. The one area in which that band had enjoyed some kind of success was in their hometown of San Francisco, where they were supported by the local promotional kingpin Bill Graham. Until the early 1970s, when he temporarily scaled back his promotional business in the face of what he saw as the excessive demands for cash guarantees from visiting rock bands, Graham was the owner of several of the country's best-known theatres for live rock 'n' roll – the Fillmore East (New York), Fillmore West (San Francisco) and the Winterland

Ballroom (also San Francisco). It was Bill Graham's Fillmore East that provided the venue for Humble Pie's breakthrough live album – but also for dozens of other live albums recorded in the 1970s, including landmark releases by Jimi Hendrix (*Band of Gypsys*, actually recorded on the last day of 1969), the Allman Brothers Band (*At Fillmore East*) and Joe Cocker (*Mad Dogs and Englishmen*).

The appeal of the Fillmore East to those who recorded concerts there was essentially due to a variety of factors. Its audience, who had been primed over the preceding years by Bill Graham to have certain expectations of a live show as an event, made the venue one of the most prestigious in the country. His venues employed light shows and the best sound systems, and raised the professional standards of rock performance to new peaks, making other promoters compete with him to land the most in-demand bands of the day. To play at any of Graham's venues on either coast, for any band who considered themselves outside the mainstream, was as close to confirmation that you had made it as was possible. But Graham wasn't a passive agent in his booking role – he built the reputation of his venues on the bands he selected to appear in them, and in that sense he acted as much as a tastemaker as he did promoter, and his tastes were spread by word of mouth:[43]

> With no hype or advertisement, a band could make it just by people asking, 'How did they do at Fillmore West? How did they go down?' 'They were great, man. You *got* to see them.' By playing Carnegie Hall or being on the Ed Sullivan show once upon a time, you knew you were on your way to stardom. Being endorsed by Bill Graham when he booked you to play the Fillmore gave you the same kind of credibility in that era.[44]

In addition to the weight attached to Bill Graham's endorsement and the perception that performers had – in playing the Fillmores, for instance – arrived, there was a lot more attention paid to making the venues places where the concert experience could be expanded into a more fully realized audio-visual performance with the addition of the special effects of the Joshua Light Show (its importance in selling the bands who appeared at the Fillmore East was indicated by the fact that it received equal billing on the venue's marquee). The projectionist, Joshua White, would provide a visual counterpart to the performance, but would also entertain the waiting audience with slideshows, explosions of light and colour, and dramatic backdrops that took form as if by some kind of magic. These could expand from the stage backdrop to take over the walls on the sides of the theatre for a fuller psychedelic effect. 'People went nuts for that stuff', White said. It was the result of 'a magnificent array of things just happening and flowing and oozing' on the projected images, which were open and suggestive enough in

Bill Graham in front of the audience at the Fillmore East, 1970.

those psychedelic days that 'the audience simply made their own images up.'[45]

The Fillmore East, more than anywhere else, became known as a great performance space because it provided a better class of audio-visual experience than anywhere else. The reason that so many concert albums were recorded there was simply down to the way the music sounded coming off the stage, as the musicians would testify. 'I played the Fillmore with Otis Redding when it wasn't the Fillmore. It was the Village East Theatre', Jaimoe Johanson of the Allman Brothers Band said:

> That stage was smoking, believe me. You could walk on that stage, man, and you could hit your instrument and the presence of it was *there;* it had echo off the back of the room. The acoustics were just great.[46]

It was no surprise, then, that the era of long tours, and specifically arena or stadium tours, would give rise to its own particular artefact: the live album, or – if the record company thought it was a good risk – the double live album. The release of these live performance documents merely served to further entrench the idea of the tour, and the live performance, as the essence of what being in a rock band entailed at this point in time. And it was something that has been celebrated in numerous films, from then until now – factual documentaries like The Rolling Stones' *Gimme Shelter* and *Cocksucker Blues*, and fictional movies such as Cameron Crowe's *Almost Famous* – about a band seemingly based on an amalgam of Led Zeppelin and The Allman Brothers Band, and the groupie culture that was born in that era – and Rob Reiner's comedy *This is Spinal Tap* (1984), a send-up of a '60s British rock band who refused to just quietly disappear.

STRETCHING OUT

Of all these representations of the culture of the road, the
expanded live album – a double, or maybe even a triple – in
particular came to be seen as proof that a band had earned their
road stripes and had come to occupy a point on the musical
spectrum that was at the opposite end to the easy commercialism
of the three-minute single and the demands of pop success. 'No
gimmick, musical music – played by honest to goodness musicians
– is the latest trend in rock', ran a Columbia Records advert in
Billboard in 1969, advertising a new batch of live albums.[47] These
albums were presented almost as a statement of authenticity by
performers who adhered to the idea that life on the road was the
means to remain in touch with the traditions that rock music had,
in some strange communication of influence, inherited from
those wandering bluesmen who roamed the Delta some 40 or 50
years earlier. The often amped-up, hyperkinetic and stretched-out
performances and audience participation contained on many live
albums was testimony to the well-honed road skills of the
countless bands that had sealed their status as stage performers.

Humble Pie's *Performance* stands as a prime example of this
tendency, but for all that it is an astonishing document of the kind
of concerts that seem to belong to a bygone era, it was not devoid
of the kind of studio tinkering – the cutting and splicing of tape
to edit performances – that would ensure that the best version
of a song that could possibly be delivered after the fact was what
actually made it onto the album. In the history of the live album,
this is arguably not so unusual. Such was the case with their well-
known cover of Dr John's song 'I Walk on Gilded Splinters'.[48] In
its original version (on Dr John's *Gris-Gris* album of 1968) it was
already a longish trip into some kind of Creole 'psilocybic gumbo
nightmare', whose hypnotic effect increased the longer it went
on.[49] As played onstage by Humble Pie, it was a song that would

be drawn out to almost half an hour, featuring extended guitar and harmonica solos that took up nearly half of that time. The performance aimed, in its own fashion, and within the limitations of how a four-piece rock band could use the sound – the sonic space – of a room to enhance and enlarge a piece of music, to take it beyond constraints of studio recording. When the band cued up the tapes in the studio, they felt that 'the overall performance from the first night' of the two shows at the Fillmore 'was fantastic'. But, as the drummer Jerry Shirley later said, as far as 'I Walk on Gilded Splinters' went, 'the guitar solo performance from the second night was better'. So what to do?

> What we did was we cut the entire solo from the second night and edited it into the overall performance of the first night. The tempo was exact, the tuning was exact. It was a real stunning piece of editing.[50]

And, like many such live documents of the era, the album sleeve gave off enough 'bootleg' vibes – in the kind of rubber stamp lettering that suggested it was rushed out after the concert without any tampering or fixing – to give it the mark of authenticity; just like the Who's *Live at Leeds* (1970), whose rubber stamp on a vanilla sleeve was undoubtedly influenced by the first of them all, the Stones' *LiveR than You'll Ever Be*.

The Allman Brothers Band – a band that practically lived on the road – were a typical example of the new kind of rock band that had emerged towards the end of the 1960s. In fact, it would be true to say that there were two quite distinct Allman Brothers bands – the onstage version of the band, and the version that made studio records. Before they had even got that far – before the records – they had made their reputation after creating a sensation during their first shows at the Fillmore East. 'We realized we were a *live* band', Gregg Allman said.[51] But to occupy the stage as a real live performing entity meant that the limitations placed on song length by the vinyl medium – somewhere between two and four minutes for singles – had no place in the band's perception of what it was about. And, in paying homage to their blues influences in performance, they also reflected the importance of the blues state of mind as an ideal for a whole generation of rock musicians who had come to prominence at this time. As was common for so many others, the blues would provide the kind of inspiration that drove them to be as true to themselves as possible, and to make something new and contemporary that was not overly marked by the stylistic touches of their direct contemporaries. The Allmans' guitarist, Dickey Betts, found – in old blues and jazz – the source of his own creativity, but the older influences were always seen as a point of departure for something that would become identified as a personal style. 'There's a thin line between admiring your peers and letting them influence you, which gets real dangerous', he said. 'That's when you have to go back and listen to Django [Reinhardt] and Blind Willie McTell, Robert Johnson and Leadbelly.'[52] As heard today on the expanded and re-released version of *At Fillmore East*, The Allman Brothers Band stretched out on that famous stage.[53] As well as the version of Sonny Boy Williamson's 'One Way Out', there were a handful of other cover versions – further extended workouts, to be more precise – of songs by Blind Willie McTell ('Statesboro Blues'), Muddy Waters ('Trouble No More') and Elmore James ('Done Somebody Wrong'). What is significant about their versions of these songs is that they became occasions for a greater freedom of musical expression, because they evolved organically. Gregg Allman said:

> those long jams just emanated from within the band, because we didn't want to just play three minutes and be over. And we definitely didn't want to play anybody else's songs . . . unless it

The Allman Brothers Band, *At Fillmore East*, 1971. A landmark double live album and forerunner of similar releases by numerous rock bands throughout the '70s. It featured performances of Allman originals alongside extended improvisations on blues songs of Elmore James, Blind Willie McTell and Muddy Waters.

was an old blues song like 'Trouble No More' that we would totally refurbish to our tastes.[54]

At Fillmore East was released by the Atlantic Records subsidiary ATCO, whose boss at the time was the legendary Jerry Wexler. As a producer, Wexler's forte had been the two- to three-minute song, and his expertise in this area had been amply demonstrated over a period of more than a decade in the many soul and R&B songs he had been at the helm of in his career, including hits by Aretha Franklin, Ray Charles, Wilson Pickett, The Drifters and many others. He was a fan and supporter of the Allmans, yet found it difficult to reconcile his idea of what a record was with the new kind of performance that was represented in their stage act. Following the recording of the Fillmore concerts, he thought that the band and their producer Tom Dowd would just dispense with the long jams captured in performance, and edit or keep those songs that conformed to the more standard length that radio preferred, and release it as a single album. He was so wrong about this that the band's manager, Phil Walden, had to convince him that the mere idea of 'a phonograph record' as the principal medium through which musical creativity was thought to exist was 'confining' to the Allman Brothers Band.[55] The live event was what The Allman Brothers Band were all about, and they could only be represented – on a live album, especially – with the extended jams preserved, and spread over four sides of vinyl rather than two.

For about ten years, until the turn of the '80s, the live album was a staple part of how record companies, artist management and the industry in general perceived artistic development. But it also became a cheap option for a quick return, if not the easiest way to fulfil contractual obligations for artists who had moved on to new labels. Fans nonetheless lapped up these products and artists were usually happy to be involved with them. And, purely in performance terms, the widespread existence of the format suggested that rock music had assumed a level of seriousness about performance and musicianship that had been more commonly associated with jazz, where the live album format had long been a staple of the recorded output of most artists.

Despite the peak era for live albums having long since passed, recent years have seen a glut of releases that aim to comprehensively document the performance career of long-established 'heritage' artists, particularly those from the 1960s and '70s. This is evidence, if nothing else, of the extent to which live recording became routine for touring bands during that era. From long-defunct bands like The Doors, whose *Bright Midnight* series has been releasing bootlegs under an official imprint since the turn of the century (more than a dozen to date), to artists such as Bob Dylan and Neil Young, who maintain a steady stream of releases from their own vaults, the live albums keep on coming and are now free from the constraints of the vinyl medium. But for the most part, these represent the surfacing of performances that were recorded in the days of the live album's 'natural' lifespan. In truth, the format as a means of contemporaneous documentation of life on the road began to fade from existence in the 1980s.

It reached some kind of end in the over-the-top form of Bruce Springsteen's exhaustive five-album set, *Bruce Springsteen and the E-Street Band: Live, 1975–85*. Springsteen was regarded as one of the most exciting and unpredictable performers of the 1970s and had long been bootlegged. He was known to drop unreleased songs into his set that never made it onto his albums, as well as numerous cover versions, all of which helped to sustain and pace marathon stage performances that could last up to three or more hours. But when he finally got around to releasing his long-awaited live album, for many it lacked something of the bootleg experience that had helped to seal his legend as a stage performer. Rather than being a presentation of a single continuous concert, it was comprised of songs recorded at a variety of locations over a ten-year period, covering different phases of the life of his band (as club band, as arena and stadium giants, and so on).

It was an album characterized and shaped by the lyrical concerns of its songs as much as by the fact of its 'live-ness'.

Yet these songs are interesting as examples of road music: their principal subject-matter often seemed to be that kind of road romanticism that had infused so many of Springsteen's songs and albums, from 'Born to Run' and 'Thunder Road' to the more recent album and film, *The Promise*. In so many of Springsteen's songs, road that had characterized the state of mind of the Delta singers was conceived as the route to fulfilment for working men and women from small towns and suburban backwaters whose existence had been robbed, not only of opportunities, but of the freedom that had seemed to be America's promise. 'At its heart,' Dave Marsh wrote of Springsteen's mammoth live album, 'it was the latest in a series through which a rock star and his cast of characters struggled from innocence to maturity.'[56]

8 LED ZEPPELIN: TRAVELLERS OF TIME AND SPACE

Rock music can be seen as one attempt to break out of this
dead soulless universe and reassert the universe of magic.
William S. Burroughs, 'Rock Magic' (1975)

TO WESTERN SHORES

By the 1970s, rock culture was encompassed and defined by the
aesthetic conditions of existence that brought the music to life –
the act of musical creation, the mastery of the sonic environments
of stage and studio, and the expectation that surrounded the
annual album releases and tours. For the creators, this music was
not a means – as it was for the audience – to step outside of the
routine of everyday life. It was there to be expressed as an element
of life itself, as an expression of that life's purpose and meaning.
For some critics, this was a problem, as rock music – by the turn
of the 1970s – was becoming bound up with its own concerns: for
a booming industry 'polluted with the vinyl flotsam and jetsam
of planned obsolescence' the aim seemed to be to produce endless
'chewing gum for the mind'; and for the performers, life on the
road was becoming everything.[1]

The band that most personified rock music in the 1970s and
the strange nature of the relationship that had grown up between,
on the one hand, the world of white rock music and, on the other,
Delta blues and '50s rock 'n' roll, was Led Zeppelin. But not only
had Led Zeppelin dipped into the whole stew of twentieth-century
American music – the blues, early rock 'n' roll, '60s folk-rock and
psychedelia – they had used what guitarist Jimmy Page referred to
as his 'CIA' influences, which lent the music an air of non-Western
exoticism (the initials stood for the Celtic, Indian and Arabic
elements that occasionally came to the fore over the twelve short

years that they were active). Indeed, as Erik Davis has observed, songs such as 'Four Sticks', 'Black Mountain Side', 'Friends' and 'Kashmir' are melodically and vocally redolent of Indian, Arabic and Middle Eastern modes, and might be thought to form part of an 'Orientalist travelogue' that ends with Page and singer Robert Plant travelling in person to record with the Bombay Symphony Orchestra in the early 1970s.[2]

But while Led Zeppelin could be argued to have thought of themselves as romantic (as well as musical) travellers, and Robert Plant, in his onstage banter, frequently alluded to many of their songs as evocations of a kind of ceaseless questing or obsession with life as 'the journey that never ends', they were exemplars of a rather particular kind of road music that had much to do with their adventures in America.[3] Led Zeppelin was a band that took hold of the idea that the life of the musician should be a vehicle for expressing personal and creative freedom – a direct legacy of the Delta blues – in ways that few others had. Jimmy Page, for instance, had the first four words of the 'faintly ominous cornerstone of Aleister Crowley's magick Law of Thelema' – *Do what thou wilt shall be the whole of the law* – etched into the run-out groove of the original pressings of *Led Zeppelin III*, a phrase that is intended to 'affirm the magical will and its power to craft reality with ritual utterance'.[4]

Led Zeppelin was the culmination of all the trends that were initiated in the 1960s – and was, of course, the one band of that decade that came to be associated with the next. They truly did epitomize the rock juggernaut that swept everything else aside on its transcontinental expeditions. Their music and image emerges from a sensibility that was in thrall to the transformative potential of movement; to the idea of being ready to pick up and go at a moment's notice. This is something that provides the context for what takes place in their film *The Song Remains the Same* (1976) – which is built around performances at Madison

Square Garden in New York City, and includes glimpses of their
offstage lives (or, perhaps, their dreams and wishes). The film's
so-called 'fantasy sequences', those dramatic interludes that
shift the perspective of the viewer from the concert hall to
places that are reflective of some other facet of the band, all
point to the significance of various kinds of journeys that are
posited as either transgressive or transformative in some way.
It is worth viewing these dramatized parts of the film as almost
the psychological projections of each member of the band
(and manager Peter Grant) and what Led Zeppelin represented
to them.

The implicit sense of transformation that runs through the
course of the film is established by the contrast between where
they have come from and what takes over them as they submit
to the demands of being on the road. Each member of the band
is first seen relaxing in more or less romantic and idyllic English
settings. The quiet onstage figure of bass player John Paul Jones
is seen at home in some kind of mock-Tudor surroundings
(and seemingly dressed for the period – perhaps, we think, *this*
is how he actually lives), reading a bedtime story to his children.

Led Zeppelin entering and leaving America, from *The Song Remains the Same* (1976).

But it seems that the real person behind the caring father is something else, as – in a flash, one scene cutting into another – he is transformed into a masked horseman who rides out to spend the night terrorizing a nearby village. Vocalist Robert Plant is cast as a knight travelling on a small sailing vessel and bound for some foreign shore where, on his arrival, he fights unknown opponents with a sword to rescue a captive woman. Jimmy Page climbs to the top of a rocky peak, during which he is transformed into an old man – a scene that compresses time and experience, or, in other words, the journey of a lifetime, into some kind of endurance test. John Bonham, in the most down to earth of these segments, is seen driving a variety of vehicles – a hot-rod car, a dragster and a tractor ploughing a field. In addition to that – and signalling the importance of the band's manager and 'fifth member' – Peter Grant appears in a guise that many in the music business would argue was, biographically speaking, quite true to fact: he is a gangster, set upon destroying some rivals in a warped English-countryside homage to the gang wars of 1930s Chicago. But suddenly, out of the blue, they are all in faraway America, driving in a motorcade from the airport to the concert.

These opening scenes condense the essence of the idea that Led Zeppelin was a band of invaders or adventurers out of some other time and place that is identified with the Old World, who would just descend on America when they wanted to have their fun. It is a notion that has been enlivened by some of the tall tales and on-the-road gossip that had grown up around the band. Stephen Davis's infamous biography of the band, *Hammer of the Gods*, begins:

> The maledicta, infamous libels, and annoying rumors concerning Led Zeppelin began to circulate like poisoned blood during the British rock quartet's third tour of America in 1969. Awful tales were whispered from one groupie clique to another, as Led Zeppelin raided their cities and moved quietly on . . . Don't quote me, the girls said (and still say), but Led Zeppelin sold their souls to the Devil in exchange for their instant success, their addictive charisma, their unbelievable wealth.[5]

These 'girls', as partly representative of the culture that had grown up around touring rock bands in the late 1960s and the '70s, were – by some accounts – little more than over-enthusiastic fans who set out to recreate a mood of excitement and a sense of involvement that might replicate the fun of participating in the manic chase scenes in The Beatles' film *A Hard Day's Night*. It began as a 'game', one former groupie said, to see 'how many bands you could meet'.[6] But within a few years it had become something else, a scene that – in cities across the country – revolved around a number of illustrious young women who would become known to all the visiting bands who passed through town. The fascination with groupies, as aspects of

a hitherto unknown culture, was evident in a number of films of
the period: *Groupies*, *Permissive* and *Groupie Girl*; in books such as
Jenny Fabian and Johnny Byrne's *Groupie: A Novel*,[7] and not least
in *Groupies and Other Girls: A Rolling Stone Special Report* from 1970,
which sought to describe this new phenomenon:

> Groupies are the all-purpose girls who pursue the rock and
> roll stars from dressing room to dressing room, and from
> motel to motel . . . the tales of the groupies are often lurid.
> But beyond the sensationalism they are an index of emerging
> contemporary values in the United States, explainable in no
> other way. This is the story only *Rolling Stone* can tell, because
> we are the music, we are the musicians, we are writing about
> ourselves. It is our life style.[8]

Of note among these documents, not least due to the interplay
of the onstage life of the bands with the offstage demi-monde
of groupies and hangers-on, is the movie *Groupies* (1970), which
was filmed in the American hotel rooms of a number of touring
British bands, and during performances at venues such as the
Fillmore East. It provides an intimate and unvarnished glimpse
of the backstage world and the obsessions of groupiedom. While
the Hollywood movie *Almost Famous* – based on the experiences
of Cameron Crowe – places the groupie lifestyle within a hazy
nostalgia of teenage self-discovery (of music, of life's possibilities
and so on), *Groupies*, by contrast, is peopled with tragic and
desperate characters, often totally out of their heads and without
any apparent bearings in the real world. In one scene, following
some footage of a scintillating performance by the band Ten
Years After, Alvin Lee, their lead guitarist and singer, is caught
backstage in a downbeat and reflective mood, a young woman
at his side. 'What do they do, these groupies?', he is asked. 'What
is the appeal for them?'

An advert for *Rolling Stone* magazine in the *New York Times*, 1969.

It's a thing, ah . . . it's a way of life, which – I should imagine
– once tasted, is difficult to throw off. Because, I suppose,
to the kind of people they can meet down at the . . . eh
. . . YMCA, YWCA or what, groups are pretty interesting . . .
I've never heard anybody say what they get out of it. They
just get that way of life, and they're involved with . . . and
I suppose there's some form of serialistic glamour attached
to it all.[9]

There would be a hierarchy of groupies – so-called 'supergroupies'
– and a hierarchy of bands. The British bands, in particular, were
preferred. 'When Led Zeppelin was due to hit town', Pamela Des
Barres wrote in her famous memoir *I'm with the Band*:

The groupie section went into the highest gear imaginable;
you could hear garter belts sliding up young thighs all over
Hollywood. LZ was a formidable bunch, disguised in velvets
and satins, epitomizing The Glorious English Pop Star to
perfection.[10]

But despite the tales of excess that seem to dominate the accounts
of Led Zeppelin's American tours, the band had another kind of
impact that was more important in revolutionizing the business
and practice of touring, and it had much to do with the air of
power and menace that – in the eyes of some – they were able
to carry with them.

In their early days, though, Led Zeppelin's achievements
in breaking the U.S. were down to dogged persistence, if not
a conviction that the way they had decided to set about doing
things would inevitably result in triumph. The prime movers
behind the creation of Led Zeppelin – those who effectively
established the grounds on which they would remake the
relationship between the artist-musician and the other players

in the music industry – were Jimmy Page and Peter Grant. Grant was a one-time wrestler, bouncer and aspiring actor who had got his start in the London music business in the early 1960s, driving around bands including The Nashville Teens as well as visiting American rock 'n' rollers. He had already been involved with Page in the latter days of The Yardbirds (the band that Page had joined in 1966) after becoming the band's manager in 1967, and had by then established a reputation as someone who took a 'fiendish pleasure in offering his personal, physical protection' to the acts he looked after.[11] But he also became the one of the most astute operators the music business had ever seen up to that point, running rings around the moguls of the New York record business as he made sure Page and Led Zeppelin were signed up to one of the most lucrative and artist-friendly deals that had ever been made.

Before Led Zeppelin was even under contract to Atlantic Records, Grant and Page had financed the recording of their debut album (produced by Page). Once it was completed, they took it to Atlantic Records supremos Ahmet Ertegün and Jerry Wexler in New York, who immediately signed the band.[12] But while Ertegün would become close to the band – often travelling with them on tour when they were in America – neither he nor Wexler were allowed to interfere in what they were doing on their records. In fact, they never knew 'what kind of material Zeppelin was recording' until the tapes landed on their desks.[13] The band also controlled all other aspects of how they were presented, including publicity materials and album cover art, two facets of their identity that were crucial in shaping how the audience might perceive them. On their fourth album, which had no official title, they demanded that all trace of it being the new Led Zeppelin album be removed from the packaging. This, from the point of view of a record company promotions department, was insane; but it was the will of the band, and it worked in helping Led

Zeppelin to be seen as a kind of cult band that appealed to those initiates with inside knowledge.

Back in 1968, Peter Grant had also already established production and publishing companies to ensure a level of artistic control over the music that was unknown at that time. It meant that from the very beginning Jimmy Page, and ultimately the other members of the band, were 'responsible for every creative aspect of their careers, from record production right through to publicity'.[14] The combination of seasoned London session players (Page and Jones) and relatively inexperienced club musicians from the Midlands (Plant and Bonham) only became a real unit through the unrelenting roadwork of 1968–9.

From their beginnings in October 1968 (in the first two months they were billed as the New Yardbirds), Led Zeppelin had – in just over a year – completed four tours of North America, and performed a total of 106 shows. This was in addition to the further five shorter tours that took in 68 shows in the UK, Europe and Scandinavia. The guiding principle behind all of this work seemed to be simple – they would bludgeon their way to the top by ignoring the conventional route to success of releasing singles to gain exposure through pop radio. Instead they would establish new rules, build a new audience that would seal their reputation as a stage band, from which the more conventional measure of success – record sales – would follow.

During these trips across North America, and back and forth to Europe, the band's second album – *Led Zeppelin II* – was recorded; on the road, in between shows, wherever the band was able to book studio time. This approach to creativity was all part of an itinerant and hectic year and a half that was beginning to take its toll on the band as early as the second U.S. tour, in April and May of 1969. Ellen Sander, a journalist who travelled with the band on that tour, revealed the impact of the accelerated pace of life for a rock band on the road, and how Led Zeppelin were coping with the fact that they had become, almost overnight, the fastest-rising band in America. Touring, she observed, was enough in itself to force any musician into all manner of strange and extreme behaviour, simply in order to cope with the disorientation they were experiencing.

ON THE JOURNEY THAT NEVER ENDS

As was the case with other musicians on tour, to be on the road amid the climate and expectations of the late 1960s was to exist in a different kind of time-space – it was a mobile world that transformed itself in ways that were unknown to those who lived the humdrum existence of normality. Touring bands were at once connected to the real everyday life of others – and rubbed up against it often enough to be reminded of the fact – but also became acutely aware that they were set apart from it, and without the grounding that place – and home, as the place one typically belongs to – normally provides. 'Geography had been ripped past them at an unbelievable rate', Sander wrote:

> So many time zones had been crossed and double crossed that the date, even the time, became irrelevant. The road manager kept it all together in between his own schedule for sexual sorties. He arranged reservations, arrival times, picking up money, waking the lads up in time . . . 'How much time till the gig?' was the only question the group ever cared about at that point.[15]

As John Paul Jones later recalled, it was all such a blur that the main thing he could remember was how relentless the touring of that period had been. 'We worked like dogs', he said. 'There was *constant* touring.'[16]

But Led Zeppelin began by conforming to the existing ways of doing things. Like most of the new English bands touring North America for the first time, they wound up in the hands of Frank Barsalona's Premier agency. They also began by opening for the more established bands doing the rounds of the prestigious venues. In some places they were playing for as little as $200 a night (in 1968 The Yardbirds – a band then on the wane – had been taking in more than ten times that per night). But it was all carefully planned by Peter Grant, who took advantage of the knowledge he had gained road-managing the likes of The Yardbirds and The Animals in the U.S. The key thing, in his mind, was to be aware

Led Zeppelin's Robert Plant, 1969.

that certain cities and venues would be more likely to keep the momentum going and garner the interest of press and radio. It was a strategy that had clearly worked when their debut album, *Led Zeppelin*, broke into the American Top 10 – after steadily climbing the chart over the year – in May 1969.

Because there was no real nationwide infrastructure to support the new kind of touring that bands like Led Zeppelin began to establish, dates tended to be concentrated in particularly influential markets on the East and West coasts, and at places like Bill Graham's Fillmores East and West, which were more prestigious gigs both for established bands and those on the way up. Some of the best venues were operated by the new breed of promoters, who were trying to do something new with rock shows; but in some of the out-of-the-way places it was like stepping back into the 1950s, with niceties to be observed and local dignitaries to please.

In Minneapolis, Led Zeppelin had to present themselves at a party thrown by the promoter, as was customary after a show in the town, and found themselves in a 'country house, full of locals in blazers and party dresses who gaped at the group for several unbearable hours'.[17] During longer sequences of shows they were able to combat the boredom of all this by looking forward to the evening shows, which at least offered a glimpse of the momentum the band were gathering in the growing audiences who were becoming more fervent about the music. Led Zeppelin – it seems – had come along at just the right time and managed to hit a strange nerve with young people across the country, something that the *Los Angeles Times* opined had much to do with how well the music went with the recreational drugs that were becoming popular with teenagers of the day; 'barbiturates and amphetamines, drugs that render their users most responsive to crushing volume and ferocious histrionics' served up by the band.[18]

But on the days in between, when they had to traverse large distances to get to the next show, boredom and – for some – homesickness always loomed. In his capacity as bandleader and producer, Jimmy Page was responsible for delivering the next Led Zeppelin album to Atlantic Records for release by October, and he decided to grab any opportunity to take the band into the studio. As a result, *Led Zeppelin II* was an album pulled together on the road – songs were written in hotel rooms, in transit, and laid down in quickly convened sessions in the UK and North America. The tracks were cut in nine separate studios, located in New York (four different studios), Los Angeles (two), London (two) and Vancouver (one). The recording engineer Eddie Kramer, who had worked on some of Jimi Hendrix's later albums, was enlisted to run the boards for the band's New York studio sessions. These fell in between gigs and promotional activities, and ended up in whatever studios happened to be available. 'I think they'd [already] cut some tracks in England and one in Vancouver', Kramer said. 'They travelled around with this bloody great steamer trunk full of all the tapes, and they schlepped that thing around from pillar to post.'[19] Soon after its release, *Led Zeppelin II* topped the U.S. charts (as well as charts in the UK and around the world). Its success was instrumental to their ability to operate on their own terms, and allowed the band to shift the ground on which touring in North America, in particular, had been established. Within a few years they were breaking the U.S. box office records set by The Beatles and The Rolling Stones.

Touring, Led Zeppelin-style, could not have been more different from the kind of package tours of the 1960s that first introduced British bands to the U.S. Soon after their elevation to headliner status they started to dispense altogether with support bands, and were billing concerts as 'An Evening with Led Zeppelin – Full Two-and-a Half Hour Show'. By the time of their third U.S. tour in July 1969, they had moved from theatres into sports arenas

John Paul Jones, John Bonham, Jimmy Page and Robert Plant pose in front of their private airliner *The Starship*, 1973.

(venues like the Los Angeles Forum or Madison Square Gardens in New York, which could hold audiences of 10,000–20,000 people).

Coinciding with this, Grant had implemented the practice whereby the band received an unprecedented percentage guarantee of gate receipts – a take-it-or-leave-it deal that gave Led Zeppelin 90 per cent of the takings, and the promoter 10 per cent, out of which the promoters' expenses and drastically reduced profits were to be paid and made. Grant's reasoning was simple – and devastating – in laying bare the mechanism through which artists and performers had been exploited beyond reason for years: the band were the attraction that sold tickets, and Led Zeppelin were, by the time of their second album, such a huge draw that they didn't need to be promoted in any conventional sense. Announce the dates, Grant told the promoters, and they would sell out faster than the takings could be counted; and the reduced cut for the promoter would still be 10 per cent of a very big number for little work.[20]

By the time of their tour of America in 1973, Led Zeppelin were basing themselves in cities like Chicago and Los Angeles, from where they could fly out to concerts that were within a short commuting distance, returning after performances to 'a familiar hotel, instead of the disorientating jump from one motel to another'.[21] The customized plane that they used – known as *The Starship* – featuring their name emblazoned on the side, had also served the same purpose at other times for Deep Purple and Elton John. This converted Boeing 720B jetliner had been turned into 'a forty-seat luxury plane decorated in Las Vegas lounge style with a long bar, video screens, plush chairs, bedrooms with fake fireplaces and showers, all the home comforts'.[22]

If Los Angeles, in particular, would become Zeppelin's home from home, it would also be true to say that when they arrived the circus came to town to greet them as the returning heroes – as the band and its entourage took up residence on entire floors of the Continental Hyatt House hotel on Sunset Boulevard (the inspiration for the Hyatt House scenes in *Almost Famous*), they were surrounded by a motley assortment of LA musicians, hangers-on, groupies and dealers in a scene that was described in the kind of language that pointedly signalled disapproval – it was 'degenerate', 'debauched' and 'sick'.[23] Not only were Led

The entourage arrives at the Sunset Hyatt House to greet the band. A scene from Cameron Crowe's *Almost Famous* with Kate Hudson as groupie Penny Lane.

Zeppelin far from alone in indulging in all the excesses of the time, but Los Angeles – and the Hollywood music scene in particular – was itself the model of rock decadence.[24] They were tourists who partook of what was going around, just as David Bowie, Iggy Pop and other mid-1970s residents of the city did.

Where Led Zeppelin's excesses were unique, was onstage – in their single-act live show, which could round out at over three hours. It eventually found the space it needed to fully spread out in the large outdoor sports stadiums that increasingly became used as rock music venues in the 1970s. For some music industry veterans, such as Bill Graham, Led Zeppelin were at the forefront of a particularly bad development in the business and culture of rock music; one where success led to a kind of insatiable greed. 'Rock and roll had started in the clubs and the streets and the parks', Graham wrote, referring in part to the free concerts he had staged in San Francisco's Golden Gate Park:

Then it became a game of supply and demand. As the market price went up, the negotiations got heavier . . . it got to the point where bands were earning money far beyond their wildest dreams. Musicians [in the 1970s] realized, 'God, I can have a *second* car. I can have a home in the *country*. I can have a *sailboat*. I can have *everything* I want.' What else did they need? The *time* to enjoy all these things. Because the road was always the same, the conclusion they reached was, 'I need to make more money in *less* time.' Result? Stadiums.[25]

Bill Graham might have been describing those opening scenes of Led Zeppelin's film *The Song Remains the Same*, where the band are seen at rest and play in the countryside, enjoying the fruits of their stardom away from the madness of life on the road. If Led Zeppelin were the most successful band of their time, establishing total artistic control on the back of the fact that they conquered America through relentless touring, it was a sign of the times. The position they had achieved seemed to be in direct contrast to the fate that befell the stars of previous generations, including the most commercially successful rock 'n' roll performer of them all, in terms of record sales, at least: Elvis Presley.

Elvis had been largely eclipsed as an icon of rock culture by the new generation of musicians who followed in the wake of the global success of The Beatles and The Rolling Stones. By the 1970s, when Led Zeppelin were at their peak, Presley seemed to have wound up at the end of another road – one that had led to the dead end of artistic creativity, in Las Vegas. Unsurprisingly, given the city's status as a dream world of obscene and unreal proportions, he had ended up as an exaggerated and white-suited cabaret ghost of the original or 'authentic' Elvis that had so inspired Led Zeppelin (an early 1970s UK reissue of his original Sun Records singles contained liner notes by the journalist Ray Coleman, who dedicated the album to the members of Zeppelin

– presumably as the contemporary inheritors of that rock 'n' roll mantle). Elvis's last years as a cabaret act in the casinos were also heavily rumoured to have been tied to the whims and fortunes (mostly bad) of his manager, Colonel Tom Parker, whose illegal alien status – unknown at the time – led him to confine Elvis within the safety of the United States. Parker's fear that he would be deported back to his native Holland if his immigration status was ever uncovered also largely explained Elvis's failure to perform outside of the u.s. during his lifetime, a situation that would have been remarkable had it been any artist of a similar stature who had emerged in the 1960s and after. Parker's fear was that, if caught, he would be expelled from the u.s., and because he accompanied Elvis everywhere this automatically ruled out overseas trips. With the gambling debts his manager had been accumulating for years since the two had arrived in the city in the late 1960s, Elvis remained oblivious to the fact that he was more or less trapped on a kind of endless tour that never went anywhere – there was just the interminable routine of his Vegas residencies – as his pulling power was likely used as collateral to cover Colonel Parker's losses.[26]

The contrast between the two generations of rock 'n' rollers, represented by Presley and Led Zeppelin, was symbolized by the tension and misunderstanding that clouded the atmosphere when Presley, in 1975, granted an audience to Led Zeppelin bass player John Paul Jones, who visited him in Beverly Hills following a Zeppelin show in San Diego. On arrival at Elvis's home, Led Zeppelin's road manager – the abrasive Richard Cole, who was accompanying Jones – was still wired-up from the show. 'From the moment he stepped into the house', Jerry Schilling, one of Elvis's bodyguards said, 'he was loud and profane – packing an amazing number of f-words into everything he said.' It was a bad start:

'You know,' Elvis said to him. 'I'd appreciate it if you'd watch your language in front of my lady.' Things got very quiet. Everybody sat down. And it stayed quiet. Then Elvis decided to break the ice, and asked if he could see the fancy watch that Richard was wearing.[27]

For performers of Elvis's generation, the world that Led Zeppelin and their entourage moved in was a strange one. Rock 'n' roll was a different kind of cultural phenomenon by the 1970s. Back in the 1950s and the early '60s things were somewhat reversed, it seemed. Then, the only artists who spent huge chunks of time on the road were the ones who had never hit the big time, like Elvis had. Back in Elvis's '50s heyday the rock culture, as it would take form around the likes of The Rolling Stones and Led Zeppelin, did not exist. As promoter Frank Barsalona observed, looking back at the early days of rock music, in the 1950s, success on the pop charts was, at most, 'a first stepping stone to television or motion pictures'.[28] For Elvis, and others of his era, assimilation into the mainstream of American showbiz was the kind of future that was lying in wait. For Led Zeppelin and their ilk, the stage was where freedom could be found.

ELECTRIC MAGIC

The 1960s and '70s were a period of experiential extremes: of 'tripping out', of wanting to be 'blown away' and – of course – of living in increasingly noisy environments. R. Murray Schafer, whose studies of acoustic ecology have examined our relationship to the sound environment, has said that the 1960s was 'an exceptionally noisy decade':

Commercial jets came in the 1960s. For the first time music was being pumped out at over 100 decibels and more in rock concerts. Cities were expanding. It was the era of what Detroit called the muscle cars. Noise was being celebrated, you might say, in a number of ways.[29]

Led Zeppelin's stage show – the single-act live performance executed over several hours, and often at high volume – was one place where this kind of extreme experience might be had. But in terms of performance dynamics, it was more than just the noise the band was able to produce that defined it as an event; it was, rather, the way that the concert became the prime means through which the artist as performer could exercise command over the audience. It was this that characterized a Led Zeppelin concert as a singular kind of experience that defined the era. The difference between sound that is experienced through the medium of recorded music, on the one hand, and through the excess of something like a Led Zeppelin show, on the other, is simple. Inside the concert venue, whatever prior relationship the listener had established with a piece of recorded music – a relationship that works at the level of the intellect – is replaced by something much more physical or visceral, in which the body, alongside thousands of other bodies, is given up in some kind of public ritual.[30] What we tend to forget about music experienced in such a setting, as one philosopher notes, is that the listener does not merely 'hear' with the ears, but with the whole body:

My ears are at best the *focal* organs of hearing. This may be detected quite dramatically in listening to loud rock music. The bass notes reverberate in my stomach, and even my feet 'hear' the sound of the auditory orgy.[31]

This was something that was immediately sensed by the writer William Burroughs, who – after witnessing Led Zeppelin's 1975 Madison Square Garden show – concluded that the rock stars of the 1970s who played to these huge gatherings might be 'compared to priests'.[32] The concert was, he said, nothing less than 'a rite', whose purpose was the 'evocation and transmutation of energy', which drew the performers and audiences together into a simultaneous kind of unity. These were concerts, in the literal sense, of a *coming together*:

> It bears some resemblance to the trance music found in Morocco, which is magical in origin and purpose – that is, concerned with the evocation and control of spiritual forces. In Morocco, musicians are also magicians . . . It is to be remembered that the origin of all the arts – music, painting and writing – is magical and evocative; and that magic is always used to obtain some definite result. In the Led Zeppelin concert, the result aimed at would seem to be in the creation of energy in the performers and in the audience.[33]

What Burroughs meant in using the term 'magic' accorded very much with Jimmy Page's own views, in that it suggested that there must always be a moving and controlling *will* at work in the orchestration of the energy inside the concert hall. The performers were not just playing music, but playing with 'fissionable material' that Burroughs also identified as the 'mass unconscious'. As a member of the audience, he felt like he had been on one of those mind-expanding, ecstatic trips so much sought after in those days – leaving the concert hall was 'like getting off a jet plane'.[34] And, if that signalled that Led Zeppelin had achieved some kind of goal in carrying their audience away from their everyday cares, it was merely one episode of what, for the band, who were also caught up in the event, was an extended bout of disorientation. As Page revealed to Burroughs during their interview the day after the concert, it was not only the audience who lost themselves – the lasting effect of the accumulation of extended performances that

Jimmy Page of Led Zeppelin filmed using a violin bow to produce sound effects during a 1973 performance of 'Dazed and Confused' (featured in the film *The Song Remains the Same*).

made up these intense periods of touring, being away from home and living in accelerated circumstances, was a kind of physical and mental trauma. 'I came back from the last tour and I didn't know where I was . . . the only thing I could relate to was the instrument onstage', Page said. 'I was just totally and completely spaced out.'[35]

From the audience perspective, though, what happened in the concert hall could be seen as an extension of the kind of power that Jimmy Page and the other members of Led Zeppelin managed to exert in other spheres of activity (the unparalleled record advances, the power over promoters and so on). Onstage, everything was orchestrated by the guitarist and his fondness for developing a performance that showed his ability to play around with the dynamics of sound and volume, working through elements of what he termed 'light and shade' to add a kind of depth and perspective to the songs that, in performance, and with the reputation they carried on the road, gave the band a great hold over audiences. It was more than just the sound, more than mere volume, Eddie Kramer, the band's sound engineer on *Led Zeppelin II*, said: 'The ability to go from extremely quiet low

dynamics to an immensely powerful rush of noise carries a tremendous amount of weight.'[36]

As the band's producer and as a veteran of hundreds of studio recording sessions in his pre-Led Zeppelin days, Page had always understood the relation between sound and the context within which music was performed and heard or reproduced. In the decades since Led Zeppelin folded, he has continued to curate their recorded legacy through the emergence of new technologies and media, always with a view to finding the perfect sonic representation of his creations. Onstage, he was the bandleader too – with the other players following his cues, as he sometimes stretched and bent songs that were well known in their studio versions out of shape. The power he was able to exert over what – in the concert setting – was a captive audience, is there to see in the film *The Song Remains the Same* (1976), especially during two sections of the performance that is captured in that film. First, there's the long theremin section of 'Dazed and Confused', which is not merely an example of performance as the unrepeatable, one-off event so characteristic of live performance in these times, but a demonstration of the brutal effectiveness of amplified electronic sound. Page's command of the concert space allows him to move and manipulate the sound that the theremin, in a sense, allows to be snatched out of nothing, pushing it around the auditorium and creating a unique aural space. The second example is during a guitar solo where Page, again looking more like a magician than a musician, waves a violin bow around his head, slapping and sawing against the strings of his Gibson Les Paul guitar, whose amplified sound is further processed with heavy doses of echo. The effect is eerie and unnatural (some may say 'evil') sounding. These tools and effects, which heighten the sense of Page as the conductor able to command the chaos that seems always about to break out around him, also 'extended the virtuosity associated with the guitar hero into the domain of techno-acoustic experimentation'.[37]

This was all part of the use of noise and amplification as instruments in themselves, which was a direct outcome of the culture of touring that emerged in the late 1960s. As the musicologist Robert Walser has suggested, certain forms of music that rely on amplification and other means of sound processing, such as heavy metal (of which Led Zeppelin are often regarded as progenitors), lend sound a power that appears to 'extend infinitely' in the performance space:

> This spatiality complements the intense physicality of what is aptly called 'heavy metal,' a materiality paradoxically created by sound, but sound so loud as to conflate inner and outer realities for the audience. Both extreme volume and artificially produced aural indicators of space allow the music to transform the actual location of the listener.[38]

The road, in '70s rock, is thus not just defined by the time and space travelled by the performers on tour, but also by these spaces that permit a new kind of experience for audiences and performers, which – as William Burroughs observed – destroys the hold of everyday reality for those few hours during which the event unfolds. The roots of all this – this move into extremes – goes back, in many ways, to the rise of the electric guitar itself and the way it inspired revolutions in amplification as the demands of touring and playing before larger audiences became more pressing. Electric blues and early rock 'n' roll, after all, had taken 'the guitar away from being a backing instrument', to put it up front and centre as the lead instrument.[39] This made the electric guitar 'the catalyst for heavier riff-based songs', pioneered by performers like Led Zeppelin:

> Rock 'n' roll is the first musical form that consistently works with loudness: this was music to be played loud . . . [and] in the songs, repetition, both musical and lyrical would force home whatever message a song had.[40]

Led Zeppelin, while always the first to acknowledge the influence of the Delta blues on their musical development, nonetheless never saw themselves as a blues band – and why would they. Even though they often worked glimmers or impressions of those blues into their stage performances (and their albums), they were refracted through the lens of the technologies and aesthetics of a different era. For Page, 'the British blues invasion of the States', of which they could be regarded as the culmination, 'was nothing like the blues', mainly because the tools at the disposal of players like himself transformed him into 'the guitarist from Mars'.[41] His interpretation of the blues drew on the spirit of the blues and – like so many of his generation – what he had learned of the apparent way of life of those early wandering blues performers, which as we know was steeped in myth and legend.

When Page reunited with Robert Plant in the late 1990s to record their first album of new songs since Led Zeppelin disbanded in 1980, they produced an album whose title – *Walking into Clarksdale* – was more than a casual nod to the influence of the idea of the life of the road that had been the subject-matter of so many of those songs that would have been performed in and around Clarksdale in the 1920s and '30s. Indeed, the title song itself drew the link between the need to keep on moving and staying true to oneself. Regardless of the pain and disappointments that such restlessness gave rise to, to be on the road – it seemed – was a route to some kind of real and authentic experience, some irrepressible truth about oneself. The album title, *Walking into Clarksdale*, reflected the attempt to recapture that spirit, to go back in some way to the root, and it followed Robert Plant's own late pilgrimage to the Delta in the 1990s:

> I wanted to go to the Delta . . . Of course, once there was a thriving community all along the banks of the Mississippi, where the guys used to play, using boats to go up and down to the juke joints . . . It's daft, really, I suppose, going around looking at roadside buildings that have closed down in Banks, Mississippi, where Robert Johnson is supposed to have come in on a break between Son House and Bukka White, picked up a guitar after he'd been away for a year and improved beyond all recognition. Clarksdale is a very sleepy town now, but it carries a history which had an amazing effect on both of us . . . Being obsessed with that music, I just wanted to go there. I guess I was just about 40 years too late.[42]

Plant and Page returned to the Delta during their 1999 tour in support of *Walking into Clarksdale*, visiting Tutwiler (where W. C. Handy first heard Delta blues at a train station in 1903) and Friars Point, a location made famous in Robert Johnson's 'Traveling

Riverside Blues', a song they recorded as Led Zeppelin in 1969 during the sessions for their second album, as they travelled around North America inventing a new culture of the road. In the following years, Robert Plant returned to unveil the Blues Trail Marker in Tutwiler and to present a plaque to the Delta Blues Museum, 'featuring a collection of miniature Led Zeppelin album covers above an engraved plate honoring Delta bluesmen whose music influenced his career'.[43]

CONCLUSION

The music of the road was made by people who went in search of freedom, but also in search of an audience that would confirm the validity of what was – at times – a kind of vagabond or rootless existence. Sometimes – as with Delta blues – it found a much bigger audience long after it was at its most potent: recordings preserved a compelling music in sound fragments on 78 rpm discs that seemed to opened a crack in time once the needle was dropped on the disc, allowing the voices of the long dead to escape and travel in what, for them, would have been entirely unforeseen directions. At other points in time – as was the case with Bob Dylan in the mid-1960s – the pull of the road pulled the music ahead of its audience, as it reached for a future that might open up new artistic horizons.

By the 1970s, the rock music that was largely pioneered by English performers who saw in America the possibility of a new kind of existence, and which took its cues from the blues, seemed to meet its audience on the road: in concert halls, arenas and sports stadiums, and within a way of life that itself provided a glimpse of an alternative culture. The phenomenon of the live album, which is a product of that period more than any other, was – we should remember – sold as a document that preserved, in sound, the coming together of the travelling performer and their audience. *In concert* literally means together, as one.

To sit down and listen to what remains of the music that swirled around Clarksdale in the 1920s and '30s and came to be known as Delta blues – the music of Charley Patton, Son House or Tommy Johnson – is to engage in an experience that seems unusually intimate; it is unusual because, despite the time and distance that separates the contemporary listener from the source, there is an undeniable presence that demands our attention. This is not typically the kind of music that we would listen to in communal settings today, which is perhaps one consequence of the fact that the process of recording helped those who were fortunate enough to be preserved on disc to shape what we recognize as real, authentic, artistic voices that are able to cut through the 'noise' of contemporary life. It is music that – in part due to the stark directness of its setting, and often the lone voice and guitar – pulls you into a space that it opens up, and compels you to shut out your cares, your world, and enter the one it evokes.

I recall listening, some 30 years ago during the dark winter nights, to Robert Johnson's *King of the Delta Blues Singers* – then enjoying one of its many resurgences in popularity – and shutting out the lights in the room where I was sitting to more fully allow myself to be immersed in its mood, and to be drawn closer to the extraordinary voice and what Bob Dylan described as the 'stabbing' sounds Johnson produced with his acoustic guitar. It was like nothing else I had ever heard before. And unlike so much of the music of that time, which seemed trapped and canned and contained no space, no room for the music to breath and come alive, it seemed possible to imagine that I had somehow conjured up a living spirit. I felt very close to this presence and was aware that it was reshaping my perception of the view outside my window – the lights and traffic of a Saturday night in the city. It was not the kind of experience that is made possible by many kinds of music, and it was surely a similar sense of feeling connected to what was

– by any definition – strange and foreign, that turned on those who
set in motion a British blues boom that culminated in 1970s rock.

As listeners, though, many of that generation did actually
come close to the real living thing – blues singers who had been
contemporaries of the then already legendary Delta voices. By
the early 1960s they were touring England on the back of this new
interest in blues and folk music. And it was on one of those tours,
in 1965, that the teenage Robert Plant was said to have stolen
one of Sony Boy Williamson's harmonicas, backstage after a
performance in Birmingham, England.[1] Williamson had known
Robert Johnson and in the 1940s formed a successful partnership
with his stepson, Robert Lockwood Jr, performing on the King
Biscuit Hour on KFFA – a radio station in Helena, Arkansas –
where they brought an electrified version of Delta blues to
audiences for the first time. Williamson, like Muddy Waters,
who also wound up in England at the same time, was a direct
and living link to the Delta and the music of the 1930s. They were
just two of many such bluesmen – others included Mississippi
Fred McDowell, John Lee Hooker and Willie Dixon – who would
end up playing and sometimes recording sessions with the young
British blues players of that period. They also inspired or provided
some of the material that made up the early recordings of those
British bands (and, eventually, their American counterparts). On
one of those London sessions, Sonny Boy Williamson wound up
with Jimmy Page in his backing band; and two years earlier the
Delta bluesman had recorded a live album with Page's future band
The Yardbirds, then featuring seventeen-year-old Eric Clapton.[2]
On other occasions members of The Rolling Stones, John Mayall's
Bluesbreakers, Taste (featuring Rory Gallagher), the Groundhogs
and other young bands made albums with Muddy Waters,
Howlin' Wolf and John Lee Hooker.

What connects the two generations is not just a love of the
blues, or the fact that there were occasions when these old and

young musicians met and performed together, but also something about America and the space it allowed for music to become a vehicle for journeys that would inform the kind of experience that leads to self-discovery. America Delta blues musicians, and the myths and legends that had added to the allure of the music, conveyed the idea that living and being on the road was the only authentic life for the committed musician.

What I have been describing as road music takes many forms and is developed through a variety of styles. But it was music that was always seeking a route out of the ways that it, and its performers, had been confined, whether that was through forms of social oppression, creative limitations or any other kind of restraint on movement and imagination. More than anywhere else, in its later stages the affinity for the road found its means of expression in front of audiences who were primed for a unique kind of listening experience that was new to their generation, and which involved a sort of ritualistic submission to the event. This rock music, in particular – which came from musicians who gave themselves over to the road to become creators of their own music once again, onstage – belonged to an era that has now been eclipsed by new ways of experiencing music. And while it seems that touring and live performance is as commonplace as ever – it may even be more popular in attendance terms than it was in the 1970s – today audiences seem impatient to hear what they already know. Performers who were left bewildered by the near collapse of the record industry in the wake of the digital revolution were soon made aware that the way to make a living is to give the audience what it wants; and what the audience often wants is the re-creation of a music that belongs in the past, but which – due to the presence of the whole of the history of recorded music – is also of the listener's present time.

It is something that can be seen in the number of concert tours now devoted to 'greatest hits' or to performances of single iconic albums. This, in itself, is a development that reveals that the road is not a space of forward motion, but the opposite. It would be wrong, however, to say that this road music has vanished; rather, that where it once followed paths that inspired new generations of performers to follow their own instincts, it now mostly travels in quite different ways. If contemporary listening habits and the technology that nurtures them have stripped the performer of the power and control they were once able to exercise in performance (we can, after all, now mix-up and combine their music in any way *we* want to), it gives rise to a new kind of affinity between music – any kind of music – and movement, that puts the listener in control. The kind of onstage approach to music that marked the performance as an event in the mid- to late 1960s and '70s created a space in which music that was preserved on record could come alive again. But now, it is the listeners who conjure up a new kind of space of experience where the music travels without being in any sense *on the road*, or attached much at all to the idea that the creative impulse that produced the music was all about movement and transcendence. Mobile and digital technologies certainly allow *us* to move around in our own portable audio bubble, taking entire libraries of music wherever we go, but in doing so it is always threatening to diminish the music itself, by making it secondary to some other primary focus that it is now the portable accompaniment to.

REFERENCES

INTRODUCTION

1 Martin Jay, *Songs of Experience: Modern American and European Variations on a Universal Theme* (Berkeley, CA, 2005), p. 11.
2 Jack Kerouac, *On the Road* [1957], with an Introduction by Ann Charters (London, 1991), p. 25.

1 EARLY DELTA BLUES

1 Reproduced in John Fahey, *Charley Patton* (London, 1970), p. 47.
2 J. J. Phillips, *Mojo Hand: An Orphic Tale* (London, 1987), p. 126.
3 Ibid., p. 125.
4 Edward L. Ayers, *Southern Crossing: A History of the American South, 1877–1906* (Oxford, 1995), p. 243.
5 Francis Davis, *The History of the Blues* (London, 1995), p. 93.
6 See Allan Moore, 'Surveying the Field: Our Knowledge of Blues and Gospel Music', in *The Cambridge Companion to Blues and Gospel Music*, ed. Allan Moore (Cambridge, 2002), p. 2.
7 Jeff Todd Titon, *Early Downhome Blues: A Musical and Cultural Analysis* (Chapel Hill, NC, 1994), p. 3.
8 Ernest Suarez, 'Southern Verse in Poetry and Song', in *The Cambridge Companion to the Literature of the American South* (Cambridge, 2013), p. 72.
9 Ibid.
10 Robert Palmer, *Deep Blues* (New York, 1981), pp. 26–7.
11 Robert Palmer, *Blues and Chaos: The Music Writing of Robert Palmer*, ed. Anthony DeCurtis (New York, 2009), p. 59.
12 Adam Gussow, *Seems Like Murder Here: Southern Violence and the Blues Tradition* (Chicago, IL, 2002), p. 27.
13 Stephen Calt, in the liner notes to a Yazoo Records compilation, *The Roots of Rock* (Yazoo 1063, 1991).

14 John Fahey, 'Charley Reconsidered, Thirty-five Years On', in *Screamin' and Hollerin' the Blues: The Worlds of Charley Patton* (Revenant Records, 2001), pp. 46, 50.

15 This is Robert Palmer's telling of the event in *Deep Blues*, p. 45.

16 Ayers, *Southern Crossing*, p. 238.

17 Palmer, *Deep Blues*, p. 45.

18 Ibid., p. 66.

19 Marshall W. Stearns, notes accompanying *Negro Blues and Field Hollers* (L59), an LP record of field recordings from the Library of Congress (Washington, DC, 1962), p. 1.

20 Quoted in Robert Bone, 'James Baldwin', in *The Negro Novel in America* [1965], excerpted in *The Hero's Journey*, ed. Harold Bloom and Blake Hobby (New York, 2009), pp. 75–83.

21 James C. Cobb, *The Most Southern Place on Earth: The Mississippi Delta and the Roots of Regional Identity* (Oxford, 1992), p. viii.

22 Marybeth Hamilton, *In Search of the Blues: Black Voices, White Visions* (London, 2007), p. 1.

23 Cobb, *The Most Southern Place on Earth*, p. 9.

24 Ibid., p. 5.

25 Ibid., p. 49.

26 Palmer, *Deep Blues*, p. 49.

27 Paul Oliver, *Blues Fell This Morning: Meaning in the Blues* [1960] (Cambridge, 1990), p. 53.

28 James C. Cobb, *Away Down South: A History of Southern Identity* (Oxford, 2005), p. 95.

29 Ayers, *Southern Crossing*, p. 242.

30 See Palmer, *Deep Blues*, p. 51.

31 Ibid., p. 47.

32 David Evans, *Big Road Blues: Tradition and Creativity in the Folk Blues* (Berkeley, CA, 1982), p. 269.

33 Hamilton, *In Search of the Blues*, p. 191.

34 Davis, *The History of the Blues*, p. 97.

35 Ayers, *Southern Crossing*, p. 242.

36 See David Evans, 'Charley Patton: The Conscience of the Delta', in *Screamin' and Hollerin' the Blues*, p. 17.

37 Davis, *The History of the Blues*, p. 97.

38 Gayle Dean Wardlow and Jacques Roche (Stephen Calt), 'Patton's Murder – Whitewash? or Hogwash?', in *Chasin' that*

Devil Music: Searching for the Blues, ed. Gayle Dean Wardlow
(San Francisco, CA, 1998), p. 96.

39 Fahey, 'Charley Reconsidered', p. 46.

40 Davis, *The History of the Blues*, p. 96.

41 Ibid., p. 97.

42 Phil Pastras, *Dead Man Blues: Jelly Roll Morton Way Out West*
(Berkeley, CA, 2001), p. 65.

43 Jon Michael Spencer, *Protest and Praise: Sacred Music of Black Religion*
(Minneapolis, MN, 1990), p. 128.

44 Daniel Beaumont, *Preachin' The Blues: The Life and Times of Son House*
(Oxford, 2011), p. 79.

45 Fahey, *Charley Patton*, p. 16.

46 Edward Komara, ed., *Encyclopedia of the Blues*, vol. 1 (New York, 2006),
pp. 454, 456.

47 Ibid.

48 Steve Cheseborough, *Blues Traveling: The Holy Sites of Delta Blues*
(Jackson, MS, 2001), p. 106.

49 Ibid., pp. 68–71.

2 JOURNEYS INTO THE PAST: DELTA MYTHS AND REALITIES

1 Homer, *The Odyssey*, trans. E. V. Rieu and D.C.H. Rieu (London, 1971),
Book I, II, 2ff, p. 3. The film begins with a version of this invocation, which
appears on a screen card: 'O Muse! / Sing in me, and through me tell the
story / Of that man skilled in all the ways of contending, / A wanderer,
harried for years on end'.

2 David Adams Leeming, *The World of Myth* (Oxford, 1992), p. 220.

3 Marshall W. Stearns, notes accompanying *Negro Blues and Field Hollers* (L59),
an LP record of field recordings from the Library of Congress (Washington,
DC, 1962), p. 2.

4 *Anthology of American Folk Music* (Smithsonian Folkways Recordings),
compiled, edited and annotated by Harry N. Smith. The six-set CD reissue
of 1997 won a Grammy for Best Historical Album.

5 Eddie Robson, *Coen Brothers (Virgin Film)* (London, 2007), p. 242.

6 See Jonathan Romney, 'Double Vision', *The Guardian* (19 May 2000).

7 Margaret M. Toscano, 'Homer Meets the Coen Brothers: Memory as Artistic
Pastiche in *O Brother, Where Art Thou?*', *Film and History: An Interdisciplinary
Journal of Film and Television Studies*, XXXIX/2 (Fall 2009), p. 55.

8 Romney, 'Double Vision'.
9 Robert Palmer, *Deep Blues* (New York, 1981), p. 72.
10 Greil Marcus, *Invisible Republic: Bob Dylan's Basement Tapes* (London, 1997), p. 118. One chapter, titled 'The Old Weird America', is about Harry Smith's *Anthology of American Folk Music* – the kind of blues, country and folk music that is strongly evoked throughout the Coen Brothers' film.
11 Daniel J. Boorstin, *The Americans: The Colonial Experience* (New York, 1958), p. 195.
12 Ibid.
13 Paul Gilroy, *The Black Atlantic: Modernity and Double-Consciousness* (London, 1993).
14 Ibid., p. 111.
15 'Hard Time Killing Floor Blues', written by Skip James, was originally released on Paramount Records in 1931.
16 In Robert Johnson's case, the term was used in the two album releases of his 1936 and 1937 sessions: *King of the Delta Blues Singers* (Columbia, CL1654, 1961) and *King of the Delta Blues Singers, Vol. II* (Columbia, C30034, 1970); in reference to Charley Patton it is the title of Stephen Calt and Gayle Wardlow, *King of the Delta Blues: The Life and Music of Charlie Patton* (Newton, NJ, 1988).
17 Stephen Calt, *I'd Rather Be the Devil: Skip James and the Blues* (Chicago, IL, 2008), p. 100.
18 Ibid., p. 211.
19 Lawrence Levine, *Black Culture and Black Consciousness: Afro-American Folk Thought from Slavery to Freedom* [1977] (Oxford, 2007), p. 262.
20 Giles Oakley, *The Devil's Music: A History of the Blues*, 2nd edn (New York, 1997), pp. 56–7.
21 James C. Cobb, *The Most Southern Place on Earth: The Mississippi Delta and the Roots of Regional Identity* (Oxford, 1992), p. 278.
22 *Prison Songs: Historical Recordings from Parchman Farm, 1947–48, Vol. I: The Alan Lomax Collection* (Rounder Records, 1997).
23 On the meaning of the term 'songster', see Hugh Barker and Yuval Taylor, *Faking It: The Quest for Authenticity in Popular Music* (London, 2007), pp. 45–6.
24 Oakley, *The Devil's Music*, p. 60.
25 Transcribed in Alan B. Govenar, *Texas Blues: The Rise of a Contemporary Sound* (College Station, TX, 2008), p. 8.

26 Oakley, *The Devil's Music*, p. 58

27 As told to Gayle Dean Wardlow and quoted in *Chasin' that Devil Music: Searching for the Blues* (San Francisco, CA, 1998), p. 149.

28 William Barlow, *Looking Up at Down: The Emergence of Blues Culture* (Philadelphia, PA, 1989), p. 4.

29 Levine, *Black Culture and Black Consciousness*, p. 283.

30 Ibid., pp. 266–7.

31 Barlow, *Looking Up at Down*, p. 5.

32 Calt, *I'd Rather Be the Devil*, p. 211.

33 Oakley, *The Devil's Music*, p. 53.

34 John Fahey, 'Charley Reconsidered, Thirty-five Years On', in *Screamin' and Hollerin' the Blues: The Worlds of Charley Patton* (Revenant Records, 2001), pp. 47, 48.

35 Samuel B. Charters, *The Country Blues* (New York, 1975), p. 21.

36 See Benjamin Filene, *Romancing the Folk: Public Memory and American Roots Music* (Chapel Hill, NC, 2000), p. 49.

37 Ibid.

38 Quoted in John Szwed, *The Man who Recorded the World: A Biography of Alan Lomax* (London, 2010), p. 38.

39 John Lomax, correspondence from 1933, quoted in Nolan Porterfield, *Last Cavalier: The Life and Times of John A. Lomax, 1867–1948* (Champaign, IL, 2001), p. 298.

40 On the former, see Marybeth Hamilton, *In Search of the Blues: Black Voices, White Visions* (London, 2007); a more recent academic debunking exercise is Barry Lee Pearson and Bill McCulloch, *Robert Johnson: Lost and Found* (Urbana and Chicago, IL, 2003).

41 Alan Lomax, 'List of American Folk Songs on Commercial Records' (Washington, DC, 1942), p. 1.

3 ROBERT JOHNSON'S CROSSROADS

1 Quotes in Jim O'Neal and Amy van Singel, *The Voice of the Blues: Classic Interviews from 'Living Blues' Magazine* (London and New York, 2013), p. 167.

2 Francis Davis, *The History of the Blues* (London, 1995), p. 129.

3 Ted Gioia, *Delta Blues: The Life and Times of the Mississippi Masters who Revolutionized American Music* (New York, 2009), p. 171.

4 Barry Lee Pearson and Bill McCulloch, *Robert Johnson: Lost and Found* (Urbana and Chicago, IL, 2003), p. 66.

5 Robert Palmer, *Blues and Chaos: The Music Writing of Robert Palmer*, ed. Anthony DeCurtis (New York, 2009), p. 26.

6 Peter Guralnick, *Searching for Robert Johnson* (London, 1998), p. 38.

7 Ibid.

8 Adam Gussow, *Seems Like Murder Here: Southern Violence and the Blues Tradition* (Chicago, IL, 2002), p. 23.

9 Palmer, *Blues and Chaos*, p. 59.

10 Ibid.

11 On the differences and overlap between hoodoo and voodoo, see Denise Alvarado, *Voodoo Hoodoo Spellbook* (San Francisco, CA, 2011), pp. 1–25.

12 Alan Lomax, 'List of American Folk Songs on Commercial Records' (Washington, DC, 1942), p. 6.

13 Robert Farris Thompson, *Flash of the Spirit: African and Afro-American Art and Philosophy* (New York, 1983), p. 131.

14 Newbell Niles Puckett, *Folk Beliefs of the Southern Negro* (Raleigh, NC, 1926), p. 554.

15 Stanley Booth, 'Standing at the Crossroads', in *Rhythm Oil: A Journey through the Music of the American South* (Cambridge, MA, 1991), p. 5.

16 Ibid., pp. 5–6.

17 Ibid., p. 7.

18 Ibid.

19 Quoted in Guralnick, *Searching for Robert Johnson*, p. 28.

20 R. Gary Patterson, *Take a Walk on the Dark Side: Rock and Roll Myths, Legends and Curses* (New York, 2008), p. 3.

21 Quoted in Guralnick, *Searching for Robert Johnson*, p. 28.

22 Gioia, *Delta Blues*, p. 172.

23 On Charley Patton's movements, see David Evans, 'Charley Patton: The Conscience of the Delta', in *Screamin' and Hollerin' the Blues: The Worlds of Charley Patton* (Revenant Records, 2001), pp. 17–23.

24 See, for example, Patricia Schroeder, *Robert Johnson: Mythmaking and Contemporary American Culture* (Champaign, IL, 2004), pp. 1–18.

25 Paul Gilroy, *Darker than Blue: On the Moral Economies of Black Atlantic Culture* (Cambridge, MA, 2010), p. 143.

26 As Elijah Wald notes, making the contrast between perceptions of Johnson from the post-1960s to the present, and in his own time, in *Escaping the Delta: Robert Johnson and the Invention of the Blues* (New York, 2004), p. xxiv.

27 Wald, *Escaping the Delta*, pp. 66–7.

28 Ibid., p. 67.

29 David 'Honeyboy' Edwards, quoted in Robert Palmer, *Deep Blues* (New York, 1981), p. 129.

30 See Eric W. Rothenbuhler, 'For-the-record Aesthetics and Robert Johnson's Blues Style as a Product of Recorded Culture', *Popular Music*, xxvi/1 (2007), pp. 65–81.

31 Ted Gioia, 'Robert Johnson: A Century and Beyond', in *Robert Johnson: The Complete Recordings*, Columbia/Sony Legacy Records cd notes (New York, 2011), p. 4.

32 Ibid.

33 Gioia, *Delta Blues*, p. 176.

34 Ibid., p. 177.

35 Lawrence Levine, *Black Culture and Black Consciousness: Afro-American Folk Thought From Slavery to Freedom* [1977] (Oxford, 2007), p. 222. Here, when he uses the expression 'pure self', Levine is actually quoting Abbe Niles. Levine, for his part, says: 'The blues were solo music not only in performance but in content. The persona of the individual performer entirely dominated the song which centered upon the singer's own feelings, experiences, fears, dreams, acquaintances, idiosyncrasies.'

36 Gioia, *Delta Blues*, p. 170.

37 Evan Eisenberg, *The Recording Angel: Music, Records and Culture from Aristotle to Zappa* (New Haven, CT, and London, 2005), p. 119.

38 David Evans, *Big Road Blues: Tradition and Creativity in Folk Blues* (Berkeley, CA, 1982), pp. 130–31.

39 Quoted in Evans, *Big Road Blues*, p. 96.

40 Ibid.

41 John Fahey, 'Charley Reconsidered, Thirty-five Years On', in *Screamin' and Hollerin' the Blues*, p. 48.

42 Guralnick, *Searching for Robert Johnson*, p. 40.

43 Eisenberg, *The Recording Angel*, p. 130.

44 Ibid.

4 JOURNEYS INTO THE FUTURE:
FROM BLUES AND ROCK 'N' ROLL TO DYLAN

1 Francis Davis, *The History of the Blues* (London, 1995), p. 93.

2 Robert Palmer, *Deep Blues* (London, 1982), p. 131.

3   See, for example, Robert M. Lewis, ed., *From Traveling Show to Vaudeville:*
    Theatrical Spectacle in America, 1830–1910 (Baltimore, MD, 2010), and Joe
    Nickell, *Secrets of the Sideshows* (Lexington, KY, 2005).

4   Palmer, *Deep Blues*, p. 120.

5   Ibid., p. 275.

6   Quoted in Jim O'Neal and Amy van Singel, *The Voice of the Blues:*
    Classic Interviews from 'Living Blues' Magazine (London and New York, 2013),
    p. 122.

7   See Gayle Dean Wardlow, *Chasin' that Devil Music: Searching for the Blues*
    (San Francisco, CA, 1998), pp. 126–30, 131–49.

8   Ted Gioia, *Delta Blues: The Life and Times of the Mississippi Masters who*
    Revolutionized American Music (New York, 2008), p. 67.

9   Elijah Wald, *Escaping the Delta: Robert Johnson and the Invention of the Blues*
    (New York, 2004), pp. 27–8.

10 William Howland Kenney, *Recorded Music in American Life: The Phonograph*
    and Popular Memory, 1890–1945 (Oxford, 1999), p. 106.

11 Ibid.

12 Bernard Klatzko with Gayle Dean Wardlow, 'The Immortal Charlie
    Patton', in Wardlow, *Chasin' that Devil Music*, pp. 18–19.

13 For a full consideration of this, see Marybeth Hamilton, *In Search of the*
    Blues: Black Voices, White Visions (London, 2007).

14 Stephen Calt and Gayle Dean Wardlow, *King of the Delta Blues: The Life and*
    Music of Charlie Patton (Newton, NJ, 1988), p. 13.

15 Hamilton, *In Search of the Blues*, p. 167.

16 Robert Gordon, *It Came from Memphis: The Unturned Roots of Rock and Roll*
    (London, 1995), p. 42.

17 Ibid.

18 See the discussion in Albin J. Zak III, *The Poetics of Rock: Cutting Tracks,*
    Making Records (Berkeley, CA, 2001), p. 174.

19 See, for example, David Evans, 'The Development of the Blues',
    in *The Cambridge Companion to Blues and Gospel Music*, ed. Allan Moore
    (Cambridge, 2002), p. 163.

20 See Nick Tosches, *Country: The Twisted Roots of Rock 'n' Roll*
    (New York, 1985), p. 40.

21 Zak III, *The Poetics of Rock*, p. 70.

22 William Ferris, *Give My Poor Heart Ease: Voices of the Mississippi Blues*
    (Charlotte, NC, 2009), p. 143.

23 Zak III, *The Poetics of Rock*, p. 14.

24 Quoted in Max Décharné, *Rocket in My Pocket: The Hipster's Guide to Rockabilly* (London, 2010), p. 48.

25 See Palmer, *Deep Blues*, p. 222.

26 Gordon, *It Came from Memphis*, p. 45.

27 Sam Phillips, sleeve notes to Howlin' Wolf, 'Well that's Alright' / 'Everybody's in the Mood' (Sun Records SP106, 7-inch single, 2014), originally recorded in 1952.

28 Quoted in Gordon, *It Came From Memphis*, pp. 45–6.

29 There is a facsimile of the page from the Yearbook in *The Bob Dylan Scrapbook, 1956–1966* (New York, 2005), p. 48.

30 Michael Gray, *The Bob Dylan Encyclopedia* (New York, 2006), p. 684.

31 John Tytell, *Naked Angels: Kerouac, Ginsberg, Burroughs* (New York, 1991), p. 20.

32 Sharon Monteith, *American Culture in the 1960s* (Edinburgh, 2008), p. 41.

33 The programme is reproduced as an insert in *The Bob Dylan Scrapbook*, p. 21.

34 Bob Dylan, *Chronicles: Volume One* (London, 2004), p. 8.

35 Ibid., p. 282.

36 Monteith, *American Culture in the 1960s*, p. 43.

37 David Dalton, *Who is that Man? In Search of the Real Bob Dylan* (New York, 2012), p. 2.

38 Ibid., p. 3.

39 Christopher Gair, *The American Counterculture, 1945–1975* (Edinburgh, 2007), p. 170.

40 Reproduced in *The Bob Dylan Scrapbook*, p. 48.

41 Quoted in Fred Goodman, *The Mansion on the Hill: Dylan, Young, Geffen, Springsteen and the Head-on Collision of Rock and Commerce* (New York, 1988), p. 8.

42 Robert Polito, 'Highway 61 Revisited (1965)', in *The Cambridge Companion to Bob Dylan*, ed. Kevin J. H. Dettmar (Cambridge, 2009), p. 138.

43 Quoted in Clinton Heylin, *Revolution in the Air: The Songs of Bob Dylan, 1957–1974* (Chicago, IL, 2009), p. 246.

44 Gray, *The Bob Dylan Encyclopedia*, p. 531.

45 Clinton Heylin, *Still on the Road: The Songs of Bob Dylan*, vol. II: 1974–2008 (London, 2010), p. 118.

5 JIM MORRISON'S HIGHWAY TO OBLIVION

1 Joan Didion, *The White Album* [1979] (New York, 1990), p. 22.

2 The Doors, *Three Hours for Magic: The Jim Morrison Story* [Audio 3 ×LP, Wavelength Records] (London, 1982). Morrison's desire to disappear after the success of 'Light My Fire' is recounted on LP 1 from 3:00–4:55 mins.

3 James Riordan and Jerry Prochnicky, *Break on Through: The Life and Death of Jim Morrison* (London, 1991), p. 17.

4 Ray Manzarek, *The Doors: Myth and Reality, Vol. 1* [Audio CD, Fuel Records] (Orlando, FL, 2006), track 3, 'Jim and Ray form The Doors'.

5 Jeff Weiss, '*LA Woman* was The Doors' Bluesy Masterpiece, and Jim Morrison's Kiss-off to LA', *LA Weekly*, 12 January 2012. A very witty article – go back to it for the description of Morrison on the cover of the album: 'the psychic unrest of *LA Woman* is prominently placed on the album cover, which drops in April '71. Morrison is shunted off to the side like a dwarf Russian woodcutter or an American werewolf about to ruin Paris.'

6 See Riordan and Prochnicky, *Break on Through*, p. 74.

7 Ibid.

8 See Douglas Cazaux Sackman, *Orange Empire: California and the Fruits of Eden* (Berkeley, CA, 2003); on Southern California's boosters, see Mike Davis, *City of Quartz: Excavating the Future in Los Angeles* (London, 1990), pp. 24–30.

9 Kevin Starr, *Inventing the Dream: California through the Progressive Era* (Oxford, 1985), p. 334.

10 Ibid.

11 Davis, *City of Quartz*, p. 38

12 Barney Hoskyns, *Waiting for the Sun: The Story of the Los Angeles Music Scene* (London, 1996), p. 155.

13 The film clip in which Morrison first says this was on the black-and-white European tour film – but it appears in almost all the documentaries about the band.

14 W. T. Lhamon, Jr, *Deliberate Speed: The Origins of a Cultural Style in the American 1950s* (Cambridge, MA, 2002), p. 9.

15 Ibid.

16 Gerald W. Haslam, *Workin' Man Blues: Country Music in California* (Berkeley, CA, 1999), p. 64.

17 Track 9 on *LA Woman*, Elektra Records (Los Angeles, CA, 1970).

18 Riordan and Prochnicky, *Break on Through*, pp. 30–31.

19 Robby Krieger, quoted in Alan Paul, 'The Doors of Perception', *Revolver*, 1 (New York, 2000), available at www.rocksbackpages.com, accessed 21 November 2014.
20 Stephen Davis, *Jim Morrison: Life, Death, Legend* (London, 2004), p. 227.
21 Ibid.
22 Ibid., p. 308.
23 Steve Rosen, 'The Doors: An Interview with Ray Manzarek', *Sounds* (22 December 1973), available at www.rocksbackpages.com, accessed 21 November 2014.
24 John Densmore, quoted in Alan Paul, 'The Doors of Perception'.
25 David Cavanagh, 'The Doors: This Way Out . . . *LA Woman* and the Last Rites of Jim Morrison', *Uncut*, 172 (September 2011), p. 44.
26 Blair Jackson, 'The Doors: Paul Rothchild', *BAM* (3 July 1981), available at www.waiting-forthe-sun.net, accessed 21 November 2014.
27 Didion, *The White Album*, p. 23.
28 Cavanagh, 'The Doors', p. 44.
29 Ibid.
30 Riordan and Prochnicky, *Break on Through*, p. 36.
31 Quoted in *Mr Mojo Risin': The Story of 'LA Woman'* [DVD/Blu-ray] (London, 2012), from 21:05–21:24 mins.
32 Reyner Banham, *Los Angeles: The Architecture of Four Ecologies* (London, 1971), p. 213.
33 Joan Didion, *Play It as It Lays* (New York, 1970), p. 14.
34 Erik Davis, *The Visionary State: A Journey through California's Spiritual Landscape* (San Francisco, CA, 2006), p. 184.
35 David Thomson, *In Nevada: The Land, the People, God, and Chance* (London, 1999), p. 33.
36 Jim Morrison, *Wilderness: The Lost Writings of Jim Morrison* (London, 1990), p. 198.
37 Max Bell, '*LA Woman* and the Last Days of Jim Morrison', *Classic Rock*, 148 (August 2010), p. 49.
38 'Self Interview', in Morrison, *Wilderness*, p. 2.

6 ROLLING STONES, THROUGH THE LOOKING-GLASS

1 Mick Jagger in *Crossfire Hurricane* (2012), dir. Brett Morgen (at approx. 1 hr 18 mins).
2 Stanley Booth, *The True Adventures of the Rolling Stones* (London, 1985), p. 299.

3 Keith Richards, *Life* (London, 2010), p. 326.
4 Terry Southern, 'Riding the Lapping Tongue', *Saturday Review*,
   12 August 1972, p. 26.
5 Richards, *Life*, p. 336.
6 Charlie Watts, in *25x: The Continuing Adventures of the Rolling Stones*,
   dir. Nigel Finch, CBS Music Video Enterprises (Los Angeles, CA, 1989).
7 Robert Greenfield, *Stones Touring Party: A Journey through America with
   the Rolling Stones* (London, 2010), p. 52.
8 Ibid., p. 48.
9 Jack Kerouac, 'Introduction' to Robert Frank, *The Americans* [1958],
   50th Anniversary edn (Göttingen, 2008).
10 Robert Greenfield, *Exile on Main Street: A Season in Hell with the Rolling
   Stones* (Boston, MA, 2006), p. 119.
11 Richards, *Life*, p. 300.
12 Greenfield, *Exile on Main Street*, p. 130.
13 Richards, *Life*, p. 9.
14 Ethan Russell, 'The Best of Times', in *The Rolling Stones: Get Your Ya-Ya's Out*,
   40th Anniversary Deluxe edn [CD set and booklet] (New York, 2009), p. 17.
15 Cameron Crowe and Charles Shaar Murray, 'A Tale of Two Rock Critics',
   The Guardian (20 October 2000).
16 Richards, *Life*, p. 71.
17 *Gimme Shelter* is arguably the first road movie about a band on tour in
   America to show the extent of the entourage that had developed around
   the late 1960s rock band. Aside from the Maysles' film, the other contender
   for 'original' rock road movie – although set in England – is D. A.
   Pennebaker's film about Bob Dylan's British tour of 1965, *Don't Look Back*
   (1967).
18 Booth, *The True Adventures of the Rolling Stones*, p. 323.
19 Ibid., p. 211.
20 Richards, *Life*, p. 9.
21 Quoted in Ethan Russell and Gerard Van der Leun, *Let It Bleed: The Rolling
   Stones, Altamont, and the End of the Sixties* (New York, and Boston, MA, 2009),
   p. 160.
22 The main documents of the tour – aside from contemporaneous media
   reports – are the movie *Gimme Shelter* (1970), dir. Albert Maysles, David
   Maysles and Charlotte Zwerin; Booth, *The True Adventures of the Rolling
   Stones*, Russell and Van der Leun, *Let It Bleed*; and Michael Lydon, *The
   Rolling Stones Discover America* (New York, 2013).

23 Booth, *The True Adventures of the Rolling Stones*, p. 29.

24 Stanley Booth, 'Afterword: One Half of Forever', in *The True Adventures of the Rolling Stones*, with an introduction by Greil Marcus (Edinburgh, 2012), p. 365.

25 Booth, *The True Adventures of the Rolling Stones*, p. 21.

26 Stanley Booth, quoted in Kevin Perry, 'Stanley Booth on Life on the Road with the Rolling Stones', *GQ*, 10 July 2012.

27 Booth, *The True Adventures of the Rolling Stones*, pp. 9–10.

28 Ibid., p. 3.

29 Ibid., p. 382.

30 'A Bootlegger Speaks', *Billboard*, 14 November 1970, pp. R–18.

31 Ibid.

32 R. Serge Denisoff, *Solid Gold: The Popular Record Industry* (New Brunswick, NJ, 1975), p. 366.

33 Barry Kernfield, *Pop Song Piracy: Disobedient Music Distribution since 1929* (Chicago, IL, 2011), p. 176.

34 Clinton Heylin, *Bootleg! The Rise and Fall of the Secret Record Industry* (London, 2003), pp. 47–50.

35 Ibid., pp. 24–5.

7 LIVE IN FRONT OF YOUR NAKED EYES AND EARS

1 Clinton Heylin, *Bootleg! The Rise and Fall of the Secret Record Industry* (London, 2003), p. 49.

2 Lee Marshall, *Bob Dylan: The Never Ending Star* (Oxford, 2007), p. 85.

3 Ibid., p. 86.

4 John Scanlan, 'Fragments of Time and Memory: Matter, Media and the Auditory World', *European Journal of English Studies*, XV / I (2011), p. 22.

5 The phrase, as discussed above, comes from Greg Milner, *Perfecting Sound Forever: The Story of Recorded Music* (London, 2010), p. 15.

6 Paul Hegarty, *Noise Music: A History* (New York, 2007), p. 24.

7 Friedrich Kittler, *Gramophone, Film, Typewriter* [1986] (Stanford, CA, 1999), p. 94.

8 Anthony Varesi, *The Bob Dylan Albums* (Toronto, Buffalo and Lancaster, 2004), p. 74.

9 Devin McKinney, *Magic Circles: The Beatles in Dream and History* (Cambridge, MA, 2003), p. 35.

10 Ibid., p. 42.

11 Bob Kirsch, 'Dramatic Emphasis on Live Music Recording', *Billboard*, 2 November 1974, pp. ss–4.

12 Ibid., pp. ss–18.

13 Ibid.

14 Robert Santelli, *This Land is Your Land: Woody Guthrie and the Journey of an American Folk Song* (Philadelphia, PA, 2012), p. 12.

15 Ibid.

16 See discussion in Scanlan, 'Fragments of Time and Memory', pp. 20–23.

17 Frederick Douglass Opie, *Hog and Hominy: Soul Food from Africa to America* (New York and Chichester, 2008), pp. 121, 122.

18 Preston Lauterbach, *The Chitlin' Circuit: And the Road to Rock 'n' Roll* (New York, 2011), p. 250.

19 Opie, *Hog and Hominy*, p. 121.

20 James Sullivan, *The Hardest Working Man: How James Brown Saved the Soul of America* (London, 2008), pp. 67–8.

21 R. J. Smith, *The One: The Life and Music of James Brown* (New York, 2012), p. 121.

22 James Brown, *James Brown: The Godfather of Soul* (London, 1987), p. 179.

23 Jerry Butler with Earl Smith, *Only the Strong Survive: Memoirs of a Soul Survivor* (Bloomington, IN, 2004), p. 107.

24 See Douglas Wolk, *James Brown's Live at the Apollo* (New York, 2004), on the circumstances surrounding the making of the album.

25 Smith, *The One*, p. 121.

26 The song was written by Dan Hartman and Charlie Midnight. Brown said, 'it could be about my life, with all the stuff about all-night diners and all the cities in it.' See Brown, *James Brown*, p. 262.

27 Quoted in Steve Waksman, *This Ain't the Summer of Love: Conflict and Crossover in Heavy Metal and Punk* (Berkeley, CA, 2009), p. 27.

28 Waksman, *This Ain't the Summer of Love*, p. 26.

29 David R. Shumway, 'Rock & Roll as Cultural Practice', in *Present Tense: Rock & Roll and Culture*, ed. Anthony DeCurtis (Durham, NC, 1992), p. 128.

30 Quoted in Fred Goodman, *The Mansion on the Hill: Dylan, Young, Geffen, Springsteen, and the Head-on Collision of Rock and Commerce* (New York, 1997), p. 24.

31 Quoted in Simon Napier-Bell, *I'm Coming to Take You to Lunch* (London, 2005), p. 225.

32 Quoted in Dean Budnick and Josh Baron, *Ticket Masters: The Rise of the Concert Industry* (New York, 2012), p. 46.

33 Quoted in Goodman, *The Mansion on the Hill*, p. 308.

34 Frank Barsalona, *Billboard*, 14 November 1970, pp. R–63.

35 Ibid.

36 Goodman, *The Mansion on the Hill*, p. 308.

37 Barsalona, *Billboard*, pp. R–63.

38 Dan Muise, *Gallagher, Marriott, Derringer and Trower: Their Lives and Music* (Milwaukee, WI, 2002), p. 110.

39 'Humble Pie at Fillmore East', *CashBox*, 3 April 1971.

40 Goodman, *The Mansion on the Hill*, p. 308.

41 Sammy Hagar, *Red: My Uncensored Life in Rock* (New York, 2011), p. 49.

42 Ibid., p. 50.

43 Budnick and Baron, *Ticket Masters*, p. 45.

44 Peter Wolf, lead singer of the J. Geils Band, quoted in Bill Graham and Robert Greenfield, *Bill Graham Presents: My Life Inside Rock and Out* (Cambridge, MA, 2004), p. 339.

45 Quoted in Graham and Greenfield, *Bill Graham Presents*, p. 260.

46 Quoted in Scott Freeman, *Midnight Riders: The Story of the Allman Brothers Band* (Boston, MA, New York and London, 1995), p. 88.

47 *Billboard*, 23 August 1969. A back-page advertisement for albums by Mike Bloomfield (*Live at Bill Graham's Fillmore West*) and Nick Gravenites (*My Labors*).

48 On Dr John's album *Gris-Gris* (ATCO, 1968), the song title is given as 'I Walk on Guilded Splinters'.

49 Dave Thompson, *Bayou Underground: Tracing the Mythical Roots of American Popular Music* (Toronto, 2010), p. 106.

50 Quoted in Muise, *Gallagher, Marriott, Derringer and Trower*, p. 110.

51 Quoted in Alan Paul, *One Way Out: The Inside History of the Allman Brothers Band* (New York, 2014), p. 117.

52 Ibid., p. 122.

53 *The Allman Brothers Band at Fillmore East: Deluxe Edition* (UMG / Mercury Records/The Island Def Jam Records Group, 2003).

54 Quoted in Paul, *One Way Out*, p. 121.

55 Quoted ibid., p. 124.

56 Dave Marsh, 'I Wanna Know if Love is Real', in *Rock and Roll is Here to Stay: An Anthology*, ed. Peter Guralnick and William McKeen (New York, 2000), p. 221.

8 LED ZEPPELIN: TRAVELLERS OF TIME AND SPACE

1 Ed Ochs, 'Rock Now', *Billboard*, 14 November 1970, pp. R–3.
2 See Erik Davis, *Led Zeppelin IV (33⅓)* (New York, 2006), pp. 137–8.
3 On the band's 1975 tour, Plant would introduce 'Kashmir' as a song 'about obsession – about life's obsession with the journey that never ends'.
4 Davis, *Led Zeppelin IV*, p. 23.
5 Stephen Davis, *Hammer of the Gods: Led Zeppelin, Unauthorised*, revd edn (New York, 2008), p. 2.
6 Sue Schneider, a rock journalist and one-time groupie, quoted in Erik Quisling and Austin Williams, *Straight Whisky: A Living History of Sex, Drugs, and Rock 'n' Roll on the Sunset Strip* (Chicago, IL, 2003), p. 83.
7 *Groupies*, dir. Ron Dorfman and Peter Nevard (Maron Films, 1970); *Permissive*, dir. Lindsey Shonteff (Tigon Film Distributors, 1970; BFI, 2010); *Groupie Girl*, dir. Eric Ford (Eagle Films, 1970).
8 The quotation is from an advert for *Rolling Stone* magazine that appeared in the *New York Times* (12 February 1969).
9 *Groupies*, dir. Dorfman and Nevard.
10 Pamela Des Barres, *I'm with the Band: Confessions of a Groupie* (Chicago, IL, 2005), p. 152.
11 See Chris Welch, *Peter Grant: The Man who Led Zeppelin* (London, 2002), p. 8.
12 On the signing of Led Zeppelin, see Robert Greenfield, *The Last Sultan: The Life and Times of Ahmet Ertegun* (New York, 2012), pp. 217–22.
13 Ibid., p. 221
14 Quoted in Paul Kendall, *Led Zeppelin: A Visual Documentary* (London, 1982), p. 13.
15 Ellen Sander, 'Inside the Cages of the Zoo', in *Rock and Roll is Here to Stay: An Anthology*, ed. Peter Guralnick and William McKeen (New York, 2000), p. 580.
16 Quoted in Barney Hoskyns, *Trampled Under Foot: The Power and Excess of Led Zeppelin* (London, 2012), p. 158.
17 Sander, 'Inside the Cages of the Zoo', p. 582.
18 John Mendelsohn, 'Led Zeppelin Plays for Forum Audience', *Los Angeles Times* (7 September 1970), p. h20.
19 Quoted in Hoskyns, *Trampled Under Foot*, p. 147.
20 Welch, *Peter Grant*, pp. 84–5.
21 Davis, *Hammer of the Gods*, p. 187.

22 Ibid.

23 See Barney Hoskyns, *Waiting for the Sun: The Story of the Los Angeles Music Scene* (London, 1996), pp. 263–4.

24 See the discussion in John Scanlan, *Van Halen: Exuberant California, Zen Rock'n'Roll* (London, 2012), pp. 32–5.

25 Bill Graham and Robert Greenfield, *Bill Graham Presents: My Life Inside Rock and Out* (Cambridge, MA, 2004), p. 354.

26 Peter Guralnick, *Careless Love: The Unmaking of Elvis Presley* (London, 1999), pp. 447–8.

27 Jerry Schelling with Chuck Crisafulli, *Me and a Guy Named Elvis* (New York, 2006), pp. 277–8.

28 Quoted in Dean Budnick and Josh Baron, *Ticket Masters: The Rise of the Concert Industry and How the Public Got Scalped* (New York, 2012), p. 44.

29 Quoted in Garret Keizer, *The Unwanted Sound of Everything We Want: A Book about Noise* (New York, 2010), p. 145.

30 Evan Eisenberg, *The Recording Angel: Music, Records and Culture from Aristotle to Zappa* (New Haven, CT, and London, 2005), p. 83.

31 Don Ihde, *Listening and Voice: Phenomenologies of Sound* (Albany, NY, 2007), p. 44.

32 William Burroughs, 'Rock Magic', *Crawdaddy* (June 1975).

33 Ibid.

34 Ibid.

35 Ibid.

36 Quoted in Hoskyns, *Trampled Under Foot*, p. 155.

37 Davis, *Led Zeppelin IV*, p. 49.

38 Robert Walser, *Running With the Devil: Power, Gender, and Madness in Heavy Metal* (Middletown, CT, 1983), p. 45.

39 Paul Hegarty, *Noise Music: A History* (New York, 2007), p. 59.

40 Ibid.

41 Sylvie Simmons and Mat Snow, 'Jimmy Page and Robert Plant: *Walking into Clarksdale*', *MOJO*, 54 (May 1998).

42 Ibid.

43 Panny Mayfield, 'Robert Plant Creates "A Bit of a Stir" in Clarksdale', press release from the Sunflower River Blues and Gospel Festival, 5 August 2012. Available at www.deltabluesmuseum.org.

CONCLUSION

1 See Stephen Davis, *Hammer of the Gods: Led Zeppelin Unauthorised*, revd edn (New York, 2008), p. 47.

2 Ibid., pp. 19–20. The live recording was made in 1963 and released in 1965 as *Sonny Boy Williamson and The Yardbirds* (Fontana, 1965); the session featuring Page was recorded in 1965 and released by Marmalade Records as Sonny Boy Williamson with Brian Auger and the Trinity, Joe Harriot, Alan Skidmore and Jimmy Page, *Don't Send Me No Flowers* (1968).

SOUNDTRACK

'Railroadin' Some', Henry Thomas (1927)
'Canned Heat Blues', Tommy Johnson (1928)
'Down the Dirt Road Blues', Charley Patton (1929)
'High Water Everywhere', Charley Patton (1929)
'Hard Time Killin' Floor Blues', Skip James (1931)
'M & O Blues', Willie Brown (1931)
'Cross Road Blues', Robert Johnson (1936)
'Traveling Riverside Blues', Robert Johnson (1937)
'Prettiest Train', Parchman Farm Chain Gang (1941)
'Rocket 88', Jackie Brenston and His Delta Cats (1951)
'Mystery Train', Elvis Presley (1954)
'Smokestack Lightning', Howlin' Wolf (1956)
'Got My Mojo Working', Muddy Waters (1957)
'61 Highway Blues', Mississippi Fred McDowell (1959)
'I'm Talking about You', The Beatles (1962)
'Talkin' New York', Bob Dylan (1962)
'Like a Rolling Stone' (live), Bob Dylan (1966)
'Crossroads', Cream (1968)
'Guitar Man', Elvis Presley (1968)
'Prodigal Son', The Rolling Stones (1968)
'Travelling Riverside Blues', Led Zeppelin (1969)
'The Changeling', The Doors (1970)
'Help Me Baby' (live), Ten Years After (1970)
'LA Woman', The Doors (1970)
'Riders on the Storm', The Doors (1970)
'The WASP (Texas Radio and the Big Beat)', The Doors (1970)
'You Gotta Move' (live), The Rolling Stones (1970)
'I Walk on Gilded Splinters', Humble Pie (1971)

'Moonlight Mile', The Rolling Stones (1971)
'One Way Out', The Allman Brothers Band (1971)
'When the Levee Breaks', Led Zeppelin (1971)
'Whipping Post' (live), The Allman Brothers Band (1971)
'Thunder Road', Bruce Springsteen (1975)
'Tonight I'll be Staying Here with You' (live), Bob Dylan (1975)
'Trampled Underfoot', Led Zeppelin (1975)
'Caravan' (live), Van Morrison and The Band (1976)
'Dazed and Confused' (live), Led Zeppelin (1976)
'Living in America', James Brown (1985)

PHOTO ACKNOWLEDGEMENTS

The author and the publishers wish to express their thanks to the below sources of illustrative material and/or permission to reproduce it:

Alamy: p. 57 (Heritage Image Partnership); Corbis: p. 107 (Henry Diltz); Getty Images: pp. 29 (Michael Ochs Archive), 48 (Bernard Hoffman/The LIFE Picture Collection), 91 (GAB Archive/Redferns), 171 (Dan Farrell/NY Daily News Archive via Getty Images), 181 (John Olson/The LIFE Picture Collection), 204 (Hulton Archive); Library of Congress, Washington, DC: pp. 6, 22, 38, 64, 101 (LOOK Magazine Photograph Collection), 123.

INDEX